FAITH

The meaning of the sacraments

The FAITH GOING DEEPER series

Grace Peter Groves

Joy Peter Waddell

Forthcoming

Faith and Unbelief Stephen Bullivant

FAITH GOING DEEPER

Joy

The meaning of the sacraments

Peter Waddell

Series Editor:

Andrew Davison

First published in 2012 by the Canterbury Press Norwich
Editorial office
3rd Floor, Invicta House,
108–114 Golden Lane,
London EC1Y 0TG

Canterbury Press is an imprint of Hymns Ancient & Modern Ltd
(a registered charity)
13a Hellesdon Park Road, Norwich,
Norfolk, NR6 5DR, UK

www.canterburypress.co.uk

British Library Cataloguing in Publication data

A catalogue record for this book is available
from the British Library

978 1 84825 279 0

Typeset by The Manila Typesetting
Printed and bound in Great Britain by
CPI Group (UK) Ltd, Croydon

Contents

Series Introduction vi
Preface vii
Introduction ix

1 Jesus, the joy of God 1

2 Immersed in joy: Baptism and confirmation 20

3 Sharing joy: The eucharist 50

4 Joy heals (I): Reconciliation 82

5 Joy heals (II): Anointing the sick 104

6 Joy bears fruit (I): Ordination 119

7 Joy bears fruit (II): Marriage 147

8 The end of sacraments 179

Further reading 190

Introduction by the FAITH GOING DEEPER series editor

Academic theology is in good heart in these early years of the twenty-first century: much Christian thinking is confident and vigorous; there is more enthusiasm for theology among the clergy than for some decades. All the same, the work that theologians produce is not always accessible to those who should be its principal beneficiaries: the people of the Church.

With this series, *Faith Going Deeper*, the aim is to provide a bridge for Christians of all traditions to some of what is most valuable and significant in contemporary theological thinking and writing. In doing so, the series will also introduce some younger theologians to a wider, popular audience. The books deal with central themes of Christian thought and life, starting with grace, virtue, faith, and the sacraments. Their authors aim to be clear without being simplistic, and to avoid technical terms while providing a framework for understanding the subject in hand. They are assured in the truth of the Christian faith, and on that basis unafraid to face the challenges of our times.

The writers of these books, and I as the editor of the series, agree with the point Dorothy L. Sayers never tired of making, that nothing rejuvenates the mission of the Church like contact with good Christian theology. Our faith is far from dull; as Sayers put it, 'it is the neglect of dogma that makes for dullness'. With these books we hope to present again what she called 'the Divine Drama', so that it might once again 'startle the world'. That will only happen if it first of all startles the Church once again.

Andrew Davison
Cambridge
Eastertide 2012

Preface

I am deeply grateful to all who have helped make this book happen: to Andrew Davison for first suggesting it; to Christine Smith and SCM-Canterbury Press for taking it on; to Mum and Dad for the loan of a study by the sea; and to the Fellows, students and staff of Sidney Sussex College, Cambridge, for being a great community in which to live, think, argue, worship and write for seven years. Last but not least, thanks must go to Lisa, Sam and Ben who have borne the brunt of its writing, and who teach me most of what I know about joy.

Introduction

Sacraments matter because they help bring this world to a joy far beyond its wildest imaginings. They open up our destiny, and move us towards it. They are the ways in which Jesus lays hold of ordinary lives and ordinary things and reveals them as even now charged with glory, while also waiting 'with eager longing for the revealing of the children of God . . . (for) the freedom of the glory of the children of God' (Romans 8.19, 21). Sacraments are eruptions of divine joy into this world, which will carry us all to eternal joy.

As St Paul said though, we hold all the treasures of the gospel in clay jars: in our physical, moral, spiritual and intellectual inadequacy. When it comes to the sacraments, that clayness is especially evident. Some have almost vanished from church life: most Christians in the contemporary West, for instance, have never received the sacraments of reconciliation or anointing. Indeed, there are some 'fresh expressions of church' which give the impression that all sacraments are a kind of optional extra for rather old-fashioned people who like religious rituals. In more 'traditional' churches, by contrast, sacraments like baptism and the eucharist take central place, but sometimes with rather little thought or indeed enthusiasm. Those who are passionate about them meanwhile often express that in the form of polemical arguments with other Christians: like much church history, the story of sacramental theology is often of battles and bad news and tears.

This book presents the sacraments with serious joy. It is, above all, a celebration. If it achieves its purpose the reader will want to go and celebrate some sacraments. There will be information and argument in what follows – lots of it – but this is not a textbook, designed to give full, impartial coverage of all the differing views on all the questions sacramental theology encounters. Rather, this is an evangelical book. For me, and for great swathes of the Christian tradition, the sacraments are how the gospel has come alive, how the joy of Jesus is known. They are not of course the only way, merely a crucial and central way. I am writing this book to share that experience, to hold before you a vision of compelling joy and beauty – in the hope that you will want to enter it too.

Experience is simply lived tradition, and the tradition which has fed me more than any other is that of western Catholicism, especially as mediated within the Anglican tradition. Much of what follows springs naturally from that stream. Both Anglican and Roman Catholic theology and practice are constant sources of reference and inspiration. However, there will also be respectful disagreement with both traditions, and it is very much to be hoped that Christians from other backgrounds will find much to rejoice in here. The book is written by an Anglican and obviously so, but it is not intended to be an Anglican book.

One of the ways in which it is obviously *not* straightforwardly Anglican is in making the backbone of the book the treatment of seven sacraments. Article XXV of the XXXIX Articles made it clear – as did most sixteenth-century Reformers – that there are just two sacraments: baptism and the eucharist. The other five 'commonly called sacraments' (confirmation, marriage, ordination, reconciliation and anointing) were not considered as in the same league, and possibly not as sacraments at all. The Protestants agreed with Rome that for something to be a sacrament, Jesus had to have commanded his Church to do it. They disagreed that in the case of these five that was clear. The rituals involved might be good and proper things, but they weren't sacraments.

The days of ecumenical angst about this question are largely over. The Roman Catholic Church has made it abundantly clear (and in truth always did) that it does not see the seven as all of equal importance. Baptism and eucharist are the two foundational sacraments at the heart of Christian life. The others all depend upon and point towards these two. Accordingly, Protestants have been in this respect less anxious to polemicize against Rome. Most Protestant writers now are simply not overly worried about how many sacraments there are, or indeed exactly how that number should be identified. Many are also increasingly willing to acknowledge the great importance of the five 'commonly called sacraments' to the Church.

The dispute does though raise two interesting questions. First, what exactly is a sacrament? And second, if we don't need to stop counting after two, why stop at seven? The answer to the first question is one which shall unfold throughout the book, but here is a preliminary definition: sacraments are what happens when Jesus lays hold of something or someone, and acts through them to share his joy with others. Sacraments happen when created reality becomes the bearer of divine joy, when human actions or other signs (a word of forgiveness, a piece of bread) become the form of Jesus' action in the world today. As the *Book of Common Prayer* Catechism puts it, a sacrament is 'an outward and visible sign of an inward and spiritual grace'. Through them, joy happens.

And why did the medieval theologians (who in this as in so much theology did the systematizing) count only seven sacraments? Why not six, or twenty? The old answer was that Jesus had actually instituted seven (but biblical criticism has dented confidence that this can convincingly be said of, for instance, confirmation or anointing of the sick). Some have said that it was instead because of a medieval love for seven as a symbol of perfection, a numerological aestheticism which our culture no longer shares. More compelling, however, is the suggestion that stopping at seven heeded the testimony of a millennium of lived Christian experience that these represented what the Church actually needed. Through them, people became Christians, received the ministry of word and sacrament through Jesus' apostles, were forgiven, had their love and fertility blessed, and were strengthened for death. These seven represented all that was essential to the full flourishing of Christian life, individual and corporate.

Indeed, maybe it was this insight which shaped the conviction that they were instituted by Jesus. Arguably, for the medieval Church he *should* have done so – and consequently texts were made to bear more than they could to prove that he did. The great twentieth-century Roman Catholic theologian Karl Rahner pursued this instinct. He suggested that while it was difficult or impossible to prove direct institution of the seven by Jesus, nonetheless we could be confident that Jesus wanted there to be a Church (a statement some might find controversial: a complete justification would demand another book, but this one will suggest many reasons to share Rahner's confidence). If Jesus wanted there to be a Church, he must also have willed the things that allow there to be a Church. Accordingly, implicitly, Jesus *did* institute the seven. While the Church's justification of this from particular scriptural texts was sometimes dubious, its theological instinct had after all been sound. The seven are essential to what Jesus willed, so Jesus willed them.[1]

Whatever is made of that, there is of course more to the Church's flourishing, or to each individual Christian's flourishing, than what is essential. Take iconography or music-making, both long central to Christian worship. The Christian life might be truly lived without either, but countless Christians have testified that through soaring chorus or painted wood they have been caught up in the joy of Jesus, that God's life was shared with them through these mundane realities. Equally, the singer and the iconographer both testify that through the very act of making their sign they have tasted something of the glory they point to. So both are apparently obvious candidates for sacramental status.

The mention of music, which exists well beyond the realm of worship and often seems entirely secular, suggests another crucial element of a full theology of the sacraments. Part of the richness of such theology is precisely its intuition that the whole world is charged with the glory of God, that any and all created reality is capable of becoming the form of the divine action. In this it is deeply at one with Christianity's central convictions about the resurrection of the body and the coming transfiguration of all things – the new creation. If we only identify seven now, it is the potentiality of the whole world which those seven reveal. In the old phrase, all is *capax Dei*: capable of bearing God.

This confidence in creation, incidentally, is not simply a variation on the theme found in many different religions, cultures and spiritualities: that the world around us, and

1 Karl Rahner, 1963, *The Church and the Sacraments*, New York: Herder and Herder, pp. 41–74.

especially the beauties of nature, are numinous with presence, have about them something of the holy. The Christian is not, like William Wordsworth, 'a worshipper of nature'. There is too much naivety in such a stance, too much self-indulgence and forgetfulness of nature's cruel ambivalence – what Richard Dawkins has called its blind, pitiless indifference. Nature is not God.

Yet Wordsworth was not entirely wrong. For the Christian, nature may not be God, but it is the good creation of God. It is also, crucially, where God has come to be in his Son: 'the Word became flesh, and lived among us' (John 1.14). Nature, for the Christian, is just like us, for we are part of it. It is ambivalent: sometimes glorious, sometimes banal, sometimes astonishingly beautiful, sometimes gruesomely ugly. Above all, it is mortal. Yet, also like us, it has been changed utterly by the coming of Jesus. Because of him, powers are at work in people and nature which are lifting both beyond themselves, surging around and within to carry both to glory. In Jesus, the world is charged with glory: he is the bottomless well planted deep in the heart of creation from which springs up all that makes the world a blessing, and all the energies we meet in the sacraments.

And so the first chapter in this book on sacraments has rather little to do, on the face of it, with sacraments. It is, rather, about Jesus: about who he was, and what he did – who he is, and what he does. He is the one from whom sacraments come, the one who works in them, the one to whom they join us, and the one in whom they will make us, and the whole world, joyful. He is the one with whom all Christian theology begins, so our celebration of the sacraments begins with him.

1

Jesus, the joy of God

One of the puzzles which first interested me in the area of sacramental theology is why, it seems, Jesus did not baptize very much.

Many people are surprised when this is pointed out – and there is indeed some room for debate. John 3.22 explicitly states that Jesus did baptize (although only to be swiftly contradicted by John 4.2). Quite possibly, at some stage, he did. However, it does not appear to have been an enduring part of his practice. Note the deafening silence of the Synoptic Gospels, which never mention Jesus baptizing – not even in those passages which summarize his characteristic activities of preaching, healing and casting out evil spirits. Baptism, it seems, was John's mission – not Jesus'.[2]

However, one of the most historically certain facts about Jesus is that he was himself baptized by John. It is directly stated by two Gospels (Mark and Matthew) despite being deeply inconvenient for the early Church, and therefore highly unlikely to be the product of Christian invention. To be baptized by John might appear to make Jesus John's disciple, and there is some evidence of dispute between

2 Peter M. Waddell, March/April 2009, 'Ordained by Christ in his Church? Jesus and Baptism', *Theology*, Vol. CXII, no. 866, pp. 83–91.

their respective followers about which of them was to be regarded as the greater. In such circumstances, one imagines a certain awkwardness about the baptism among Christians – and this is precisely what we find. Matthew has John protest that he is not worthy to baptize Jesus. Luke omits any mention of John from his record of the event. The Fourth Gospel hurriedly skims over the whole incident.

It seems very likely then that Jesus was baptized by John. Presumably, at least initially, he identified himself with John's message: that God was about to act to bring about his Kingdom, and that in response to this Israel must repent and make itself ready. And indeed, that confidence in the imminent action of God to save his people characterizes Jesus' teaching throughout his ministry. Why then did he not baptize people himself?

One clue lies in noticing certain other differences between the public ministries of Jesus and John. John was above all a prophet of fiery justice: God was coming, and the unrepentant wicked would meet their just deserts. 'You brood of vipers! Who warned you to flee from the wrath to come?' are his words of greeting to the crowds that come to see him (Luke 3.7). His response to the wickedness of the world is righteous rage, which strains at the leash to see God tear down all that resists his will. It is a rage which belongs in the wilderness, fuming against the corruption and complacency of settled Israel – and also a rage which brings with it a deep grief for the failure of the people. All this found its natural expression in John's ascetism and his distinctive practice of baptism which, as we shall see in the next chapter, was above all a way of expressing repentance and readiness for the coming judgement of God.

Jesus' ministry was different. He left the wilderness to move among the villages and towns, and could be called a glutton and too fond of his wine. Fond too of bad company – women of loose morals, tax collectors, the corrupt and the complacent. His conversation with them seems to have involved much more than simple condemnation, if it involved condemnation at all. He actually seemed to enjoy being with these people. What is more, he did not encourage his followers in ascetic practices such as fasting, and defended them against the charge of laxity by saying that when in his presence, the right response is to feast. No wonder John, facing death, watches Jesus with perplexity from his prison cell and sends his friends to ask: '*Are* you the one who is to come, or are we to wait for another?'

'Go and tell John what you hear and see,' replies Jesus: 'the blind receive their sight, the lame walk, the lepers are cleansed, the deaf hear, the dead are raised, and the poor have good news brought to them. And blessed is anyone who takes no offence at me' (Matthew 11.3–6).

In other words, the Kingdom of God has dawned. What John called the people to get ready for, what was anticipated in his baptism, has started to happen around Jesus. Moreover, it is happening in a deeply surprising way. The note of judgement never disappears utterly from Jesus' teaching, and it is still grimly possible for people to bring it upon themselves. But in Jesus, God meets Israel first and foremost not as the great destroyer, but as one who loves and wants to rejoice with his people, setting them free from all that is wrong in their lives. Meeting that God, the first response is not repentance and baptism, but feasting and delight. John spoke of God's justice, Jesus embodied God's joy.

The contrast between John and Jesus is perhaps best caught at the moment when the latter opens his public ministry, according to Luke. He has been baptized, and has spent forty days in the wilderness. He comes then to

Nazareth and reads from the prophecy of Isaiah words which have become known as 'The Nazareth Manifesto':

> 'The Spirit of the Lord is upon me,
> because he has anointed me
> to bring good news to the poor.
> He has sent me to proclaim release to
> the captives
> and recovery of sight to the blind,
> to let the oppressed go free,
> to proclaim the year of the Lord's favour.'
> *Luke 4.18–19*

Isaiah immediately went on to herald 'the day of vengeance of our God', and John would have done the same. Jesus does not. Sin and judgement remain, and Jesus will say and do much about both in unexpected ways culminating on the cross. But the first word and the key signature of his mission is different: it is release, liberation, joy. Others may come to kill and destroy; Jesus has come so that Israel might have life, and have it abundantly. And so, right throughout the Gospels, this is what Jesus does. He sets people free to live abundantly, and so he sets Israel free to be what it is meant to be: the holy nation, the people of God. Take a typical story from Luke:

> Now he was teaching in one of the synagogues on the sabbath. And just then there appeared a woman with a spirit that had crippled her for eighteen years. She was bent over and was quite unable to stand up straight. When Jesus saw her, he called her over and said, 'Woman, you are set free from your ailment.'

When he laid his hands on her, immediately she stood up straight and began praising God. But the leader of the synagogue, indignant because Jesus had cured on the sabbath, kept saying to the crowd, 'There are six days on which work ought to be done; come on those days and be cured, and not on the sabbath day.' But the Lord answered him and said, 'You hypocrites! Does not each of you on the sabbath untie his ox or his donkey from the manger, and lead it away to give it water? And ought not this woman, a daughter of Abraham whom Satan bound for eighteen long years, be set free from this bondage on the sabbath day?' When he said this, all his opponents were put to shame; and the entire crowd was rejoicing at all the wonderful things that he was doing.
Luke 13.10–17

There is a way of telling this story which is rather boring, which is to understand it as being about the need to guard against religious rules becoming an excuse for not helping people. This is boring, because most of us know that already. It is also rather sinister, as it easily feeds into a long-standing Christian prejudice against Jews – namely, that they are fixated on laws, whereas enlightened Christians know that love is supreme. This may conceivably have been fair comment on certain Jews at certain times – as it would be on Christians – but on the whole is deeply unfair. Most Jews, in Jesus' day as in ours, and including their officials, would have been delighted with a miraculous healing and would not have asked too many questions as to its religious propriety.

But there is another reading which shows why this story is truly *gospel*: good news. Think about who gets healed. The sick woman on two counts (being female, and sick) did not have the assured place in society enjoyed by the male and the healthy. She certainly did not belong out in front at the synagogue, at the centre of the holy people. Her place is rather cowering at the back. And Jesus calls her out before everyone, touches her – itself a fairly radical act – and says, 'stand up straight'. It is the Sabbath, and you are set free – not just from the crippled spine but from everything which presses you down, everything which tells you you are not fit to be here, everything which denies your identity as a daughter of Abraham. You are free, and in this little synagogue Israel is whole again.

Or take the story of Zacchaeus, another one cut off from the people of Israel – this time through his own wickedness in acting as a tax collector for the Romans. His activity condemned him to social isolation and disgrace, and condemned others to economic misery. Around him, Israel failed. John wanted God to scour the likes of Zacchaeus from the land. Jesus went and dined with him, and through friendship brought him back from his self-imposed exile. The poor would have their money again, fourfold, and Zacchaeus could have his people again. Over any grumbling, Jesus said, 'Today, salvation has come to this house, because he too is a son of Abraham. For the Son of Man came to seek out and to save the lost' (Luke 19.9–10). No one must be lost, no one must be left behind: Israel must be set free to be Israel, the glory of God among the nations. This is the great driving force of Jesus' life. And so throughout the Gospels he goes, smashing down whatever barriers the people of God have carved themselves up by, bringing joy and feasting where there were divisions of sex, poverty, sickness and sin. Around Jesus, in all Israel's misery, joy happens.

The last enemy, however, is death. Death is the ultimate divider, that which breaks down the people, separating them into their graves where they are forever alone, forever isolated. The dead have lost the living, and the living have lost the dead, forever. The Psalms express the fear that the dead are cut off even from God: 'Will the dust praise you?' (Psalm 30.9). Death is the ultimate failure of relationship, and thus the ultimate mockery of God's hope for Israel. And so, Jesus' mission must inevitably involve confrontation with the power of death. If joy rebuilds Israel only for it to end in death, there is no gospel but only the pain of a common and final mortality. The stories of Lazarus, Jairus' daughter, and the widow of Nain's son only raise the tension – for these, we know, will die again. In their stories, death still reigns supreme, biding its time. Lazarus still has his grave clothes, ready for use.

The great contest comes in the death of Jesus himself. What we see is the one who brings joy, who embodies joy, allowing himself to be pierced by all that is joy's opposite. Death and destruction rush in to smother and stifle life. The one who would rebuild a people is expelled from it and from the world in the most brutal fashion. 'This is your hour, and the power of darkness,' says Jesus (Luke 22.53). So the powers of violence, hatred and contempt do their worst; they pour themselves out upon defenceless joy. Everything which divides and kills surges forth to destroy Jesus. This is what looms before him in Gethsemane, why he prays that the cup may be taken away. It is also why, in the end, he knows that it must be drained to the dregs. For the contest must be joined.

What is the most real reality? Is it the power of death, which un-fathers, un-mothers, un-childs? Or is it joy, which leaps out of itself to create more joy, which heals and brings people together? Jesus dies trusting that violent and overwhelming as the dark powers are, there is a deeper truth. That ultimately, at the heart of all things, creating them, sustaining them, redeeming them, there is not violence but joy. Indeed, he is the embodiment of that truth: he is the one whose life is nothing other than the love and joy which is the deep-down heart of things. In the technical language of later doctrine, he is 'of one substance' with the joy that makes the world: with God. When death meets this, it meets its end (more of this theme in the chapters about the eucharist and the anointing of the sick).

And so, to the resurrection. It is striking that Christian writers have not, generally speaking, tried to describe precisely how Jesus was raised. There is no narrative account such as those involving Lazarus or Jairus' daughter, partly because there were no witnesses but more profoundly because the event is of a radically different nature. This is not the temporary retrieval of an individual from death, but the end of death. It is not so much described, as glimpsed or experienced. And the way the New Testament tells the story, what the first disciples experienced was not only or even primarily some spectacular visitation of a radically transformed Jesus. That element was certainly there, but more fundamentally so is the encounter with Jesus as joy. That is, that once again, but this time more strangely, deeply and wider than ever, they experienced him rebuilding Israel, bringing what had been lost and killed together again. It is no accident that so many of the resurrection appearance stories involve sharing a meal: now, as before, this was Jesus' characteristic way of making and marking the renewed people of God. Resurrection meant that joy trumped death, and joy proves it by making enemies, friends.

Think, for example, of the apostle Peter. Perhaps we think that Peter is bound to have welcomed the news of Jesus' resurrection with ecstatic delight. There's something to that: John 21 tells how, when the risen Jesus was spied waiting for his disciples on the shore as they fished, Peter jumped into the water fully clothed to race to his master. But the Gospel is realistic enough to know that in some ways the resurrection was not instantly good news for Peter. Rather, it brought him face to face with crushing failure and guilt. To look at the risen Jesus was to look at the face of someone loved and betrayed, someone who had called Peter his Rock and had been repaid by cowardice. How would that face look at him now? At best, Peter might hope for indulgence and pity, but that is not much to hope for. That, possibly, explains why with the others he's drifted back to his nets, why the apostolic labour remains unbegun. As he reaches the beach, John tells us, there is whiff of charcoal in the air – the whiff, for Peter, of betrayal beside another brazier in the High Priest's courtyard. The joy on that beach is laced with a poisonous shame.

John 21 is the story of how Jesus draws the poison. The mysterious morning of memories is not given to shame Peter, but to forgive him. That's the point of Jesus' three questions to Peter – echoing the three denials Peter made by that other charcoal fire. Jesus is making Peter face what he has done, but not to show how disappointed he is, or to seek revenge and punishment. He makes Peter face his past so that he can be ready for what comes next: the commands 'feed my lambs', 'tend my sheep'. Peter is being made ready to be first among the apostles, and ultimately for martyrdom. All of this – the Rock-Man – will grow out of Peter's past: the weak and shameful man is not cut off or despised, but loved into change. Left to himself, Peter could only despise himself. He is not left to himself: he meets joy. Joy gives him back his past not as something which crushes with sin and guilt, but as the secret beginnings of God's astonishing work in him. Once again, Jesus rebuilds Israel out of self-inflicted ruin – and that is how they knew he was risen. We will have more to say about this in the chapter on the sacrament of reconciliation, frequently known as confession.

The restoration of Peter shows the effect of Jesus' joy in one man's life. However, it is in the nature of joy to be abundant, and the New Testament knows no limits to its playing, no bounds to the relationships it can heal or create for the first time. The experience of resurrection in the early Church was of things impossible being made possible by God – perhaps nowhere more so than in the case of a division more radical than sex, wealth, power, morality, even perhaps than death itself. This was the division between Jew and Gentile, scored deeply into the hearts of both. The day of vengeance of our God, so signally omitted from the Nazareth manifesto, would have been understood by many of Jesus' contemporaries to mean the time when God would finally deal with the nations who had subjugated and defiled his people and land. The Gentiles would get their comeuppance, and Israel would take her proper place at their head. If the Gentiles were not simply to be wiped out, they would certainly be second-class citizens in the Kingdom of God.

There are occasional glimpses in the ministry of Jesus of the great surprise to come. He speaks to the woman at the well in Samaria, heals a Syro-Phoenician woman, and hails a Roman centurion's faith with the words, 'Truly I tell you, in no one in Israel have I found such faith. I tell you, many will come from east and west and will eat with Abraham and Isaac and Jacob in the kingdom of heaven' (Matthew 8.10–11). However, it is not until after the crucifixion (and then not instantly) that the power and depth of what Jesus has done is made manifest and recognized by the disciples. The history of the first Christian century is the gradual dawning – at first in fits and starts, ultimately with overwhelming force – of the recognition that Jesus has simply put away another barrier. The risen Jesus has created a community in which Jewish identity and Gentile identity still exist, but are no longer locked in hostility. Rather, they are knit together for each other's good. The renewed people of God does not reign over the Gentiles: it includes the Gentiles. Just as Jesus gave Zacchaeus and Israel back to each other, now he gives Jew and Gentile to each other: joy turns aliens and strangers into fellow citizens with the saints and members of the household of God (Ephesians 2.20).

Crucially, this new common life between Jew and Gentile was not a matter of the disciples coming to realize that this is what Jesus would have wanted, and then striving to bring it about. Like Peter's forgiveness, the unity of Jew and Gentile was something that could only be *given* – the risen Jesus made it happen and the disciples struggle to keep up with the reality that breaks upon them. That's why in the Acts of the Apostles, the most powerful evidence that Gentiles can be part of the Church without first becoming Jews (the point at issue between Paul and the Jewish Christian conservatives) comes when the Holy

Spirit is poured out on uncircumcised Gentiles. God has made his people: all that the disciples have to do now is catch up. They are not the ones in charge of this new reality, rather they are caught up by a power, a joy, which comes from beyond them and carries them where they know not. As Paul says in a different but related context, 'it is no longer I who live, but it is Christ who lives in me' (Galatians 2.20).

This sense of the lively, powerful presence of the risen Jesus is central to the vision of this book, and underlies all sacramental theology. Indeed, it is the very heart of the New Testament doctrine of the Church, which might be defined as simply the risen life of Jesus rejoicing its way into other human lives. Beyond and behind all hierarchy and ritual and structure, the Church happens when the joy of Jesus – the joy which Jesus is – comes to be the deepest reality of other lives. Lives which were hardened against other lives, cut off from them in so many different ways, become instead lives which rejoice with others. This is the mystery of Pentecost, the birth of the Church.

John and Luke tell the story differently, but are trying to speak of the same central reality. In John's Gospel, the risen Jesus appears to his disciples in a locked room on the first Easter evening to offer them peace and to send them 'as the Father has sent me', to carry on his work of joy. John adds: 'When he had said this, he breathed on them and said to them, "Receive the Holy Spirit. If you forgive the sins of any, they are forgiven them; if you retain the sins of any, they are retained"' (John 20.22–23). Note the close association between the Spirit and the breath of Jesus: to receive the Spirit is to receive into oneself that which is most intimate to Jesus, the power of his own life. The Church, for John, is the Jesus-breathed community. And this breath forgives sins – it breathes through all that kills joy, all that destroys relationships, and lets love be again.

Luke works with a different chronology, and sees the coming of the Spirit happening forty days after Easter at Pentecost. Famously, his account tells of the Spirit descending like tongues of flame upon the heads of the disciples, and of the astonishing way in which they are given the ability to declare God's work in foreign languages. It is tempting to view both phenomena as merely divine special effects, but there is more profound meaning in these miracles. In apocryphal Jewish literature, heaven was understood as bounded by a fiery wall. Perhaps the appearance of flame around the disciples was a symbolic suggestion that the life of heaven was now *here,* in this small community. More obviously, the gift of tongues shows what this community and life are about: strangers becoming friends. One might label it as among the first sacraments: a magnificently outward and visible sign of inward and spiritual grace. And Pentecost is only the beginning: the Acts of the Apostles goes on to tell the story of how the joy of Jesus knows no bounds, how barrier after barrier between human beings comes crashing down before it.

Paul was not only the great apostle of this movement, but its great theologian. His letters are full of reflection on what it means to be this new people of God, and perhaps his most striking thought is that the Church is the body of Christ. In 1 Corinthians 12, his most extended treatment of the theme, his emphasis is upon the mutuality of the body – that every member, whatever their status, has something which only they can contribute and which the body needs. Under the dominion of sin, our natural tendency is to write people off: to strip them of their ability to give and then despise them for their failure. Through joy, however, their capacity to give and ours to receive is reawakened. The Church becomes a community where people are truly gifts to each other, where we abound only as *all* abound.

However, there is more to Paul's body imagery than even that. Philosophers before Paul had compared communities to bodies and drawn roughly the same parallels. Paul is surprising and creative not in saying that Christians are a body, but in calling them the body of Christ. The meaning of the phrase has been much debated, but it is at least plausible to see Paul as wanting to emphasize as strongly as possible that it is Jesus' life which courses within the new community: not just the memory of Jesus, or his example, but his real, risen life.[3] The Church, then, is not just a collection of Christians but the way in which Jesus lives in the world. Once he had the physical frame of a young man from Nazareth; now he has the lives – relationships, minds, souls and indeed physical frames – of countless disciples. As joy surged in, through and around the young man of Nazareth, so now it does in his new body, the Church. In and around it, the Kingdom of God begins to dawn.

This begs the question, of course, as to how the Church degenerated into the evil farce it has often been. The deadliness of the Church's sin seems to contradict all that has been said thus far. Paul was no stranger to this paradox: he developed his idea of the body of Christ first of all in relation to the Christians of Corinth, whose life featured faction fighting, greed and sexual scandal. Paul's response is stunned horror at the monstrosity of Christ's body being mired in such sin, but he does not give up on the fact that it remains truly Christ's body. How to hold the two thoughts

3 J. A. T. Robinson, 1952, *The Body: A Study in Pauline Theology*, London: SCM Press is a study of enduring worth.

together? Paul does not spell it out, but perhaps the truth is that (in Johannine imagery) Jesus is always breathing himelf into his people, always forgiving their sins. They go on sinning, grievously, but they cannot change the new truth about themselves – that the deepest heart of their being is Jesus. Christians can lie about that, fail to express it, contradict it by word and deed – but they cannot undo it. Joy lives in the depths, rejoicing its way to the surface. Sin tries to choke it, but that battle was lost once for all on Jesus' cross. Joy will flash forth, and the Church that now seems so battered and defeated will, in the end, be revealed as the place of God's joy, as the body of Jesus.

To belong to the Church is to be caught up in Jesus, who forgives the past, who heals broken humanity, and who will surge in us and with us to our perfection. No wonder, as the Church reflected on this, that the question 'who is Jesus Christ?' came to the fore. Who is it that can bring life out of death? Who can make love where there was hate? Salvation seemed no less a thing than creation: it involved the same supreme liberty, power beyond power, which made reality out of nothing. This is one who is stronger than death, before whom no created thing can stand. The logic of that pointed in the same direction as the first Easter visions and the earliest experiences of Christian worship: that the man Jesus was no mere man, but somehow implicated in the very reality of God. 'In him,' said the author of Colossians, 'all the fullness of God was pleased to dwell' (Colossians 1.19). Very, very quickly Christians sensed that they could no longer think of God without simultaneously thinking of Jesus: it was as if Jesus and what was experienced through him had now become part of the definition of the very word 'God'. Larry Hurtado has carefully traced what he calls this emergent 'binitarian monotheism' (the perception that 'God' now means the relationship of the Father and Jesus) to the very earliest days of Christianity.[4] Given what we have seen of how Jesus breathes himself into the Church through his Spirit, we should readily go a little further and describe an incipient trinitarian monotheism being in play from the very beginning of Christianity.

And this takes us to the primal spring of joy, the life of God himself. Christians came to understand Jesus as being straight from the heart of God: being, as John puts it, 'the Word made flesh' (John 1.14) – word or *Logos* here meaning something like the meaning, thought and expression of God. Jesus embodies the very character of God: he is what God is, translated into flesh and blood. So our experience of him becomes our experience of God, our theology. And Jesus is experienced, this chapter has argued, primarily as joy: as the one who brings people to life through loving them, as the one who longs for Israel and all humanity to live and love abundantly, as the one who will not leave anybody behind. Jesus rejoiced to share himself with others so all might rejoice. For Christians, this became the key to understanding God, insofar as humans can. The holy mystery of God was like Jesus: it too was joy, wanting to share itself, longing for others to respond to its joy, to come alive and sing.

The earliest Christians, then, came to understand the mystery of God in two significantly new ways. First, the

4 Larry W. Hurtado, 2005, *How on Earth did Jesus become a God? Historical Questions about Earliest Devotion to Jesus*, Grand Rapids, Michigan: Eerdmans. It should be noted that there is lively debate between Hurtado and other students of early Christology – see for example James D. G. Dunn, 2010, *Did the First Christians Worship Jesus? The New Testament Evidence*, London: SPCK.

man Jesus was somehow inextricably identified with God. There was more to God than Jesus: Jesus had prayed to one he called Father, and knew himself to be sent from and going to his Father. But this was a distinction within a unity – Christians now understood the word 'God' itself as referring to a relationship, to the love between Father and Son rather than to an undifferentiated single subject. Secondly, this relationship was understood as utterly joyful – as ready to burst out of itself in celebration, yearning to bring others within its joy.

It is sometimes asked: 'Why did God create the world?' He doesn't, presumably, *need* a world. God would be God without us. That, at least, is what Scripture and classic Christian theology have always said. Does he create the world, then, because he is bored, as a kind of plaything? Again, that's not the impression Scripture gives: the God of the Bible loves and rages and weeps and forgives – he doesn't generally *toy* with the world, like the Greek Gods of Mount Olympus. So if it is not need and not boredom, why did God create the world? The Christian vision is that he creates out of joy. That the love of Father and Son wells up ecstatically from all eternity, bursting out of itself to create reality. God creates in something like the way parents create children (see the chapter on marriage), or musicians make music. Like children, like music, creation is simply the way joy celebrates itself: God's delight.

Being a Christian is about knowing that, and becoming it ever more fully. It is about allowing the joy which streams from the heart of all things to course through us, to subvert and overcome all that within us and between us stops us from being what we are. It is about the joyless ruins of sin in us being renovated and reformed into the image of God, into lives which breathe joy and grace as purely and naturally as Jesus did – as Jesus does. It is about being woven into Jesus so that his life – that pure rhapsody of joy – plays through ours, through our unique lives and circumstances and freedom, making a joy which is always different and yet always the same. Being woven into his joy is why we have sacraments, which brings us to the rest of this book.

FOR REFLECTION

'I have said these things to you so that my joy may be in you, and that your joy may be complete.'
John 15.11

. . . the more that I love in this way when I am here, the more I am like the joy that I shall have in heaven without end, that joy which is the God who out of his endless love willed to become our brother and suffer for us.
Julian of Norwich[5]

The resurrection of the body is much more than a corpse coming back to life. It is the transfiguration of Christ's presence to us, breaking through all the barriers that our experience of corporeality implies. Perhaps one way of thinking about the Resurrection would be to see it as the transformation of Christ into pure communion.
Timothy Radcliffe[6]

---

5 Julian of Norwich, *Showings*, Ch. 6.
6 Timothy Radcliffe 2001, *I Call You Friends*, London: Continuum, p. 83.

I say more: the just man justices
Keeps grace: that keeps all his going graces;
Acts in God's eye what in God's eye he is –
Christ. For Christ plays in ten thousand places,
Lovely in limbs, and lovely in eyes not his
To the Father through the features of men's faces.
Gerard Manley Hopkins[7]

Do you want to know what goes on in the core of the Trinity? I will tell you. In the core of the Trinity, the Father laughes and gives birth to the Son. The Son laughs back at the Father and gives birth to the Spirit. The whole Trinity laughs and gives birth to us.
Meister Eckhart[8]

God became human so that we might become divine.
Athanasius[9]

7 Gerard Manley Hopkins, 'As kingfishers catch fire, dragonflies dráw fláme', *Poems 1918*.

8 Cited in Matthew Fox 1983, *Meditations with Meister Eckhart*, Santa Fe: Bear and Company, p. 129. I have been unable to trace the original reference in Meister Eckhart's works.

9 Athanasius, *On the Incarnation of the Word of God*, Ch. 54.

2

Immersed in joy: Baptism and confirmation

To be a Christian is to share in the joy of Jesus. It is not a matter of believing his teachings, or following his example, so much as of having his life course through ours. The Church has always believed this to begin in baptism. This chapter will ask first why the Church baptizes people, and what it thinks happens when it does. Subsequently, one of the most controversial questions surrounding baptism today will be addressed: *who* should be baptized? Adult believers only, the children of believers only, or all for whom baptism is sought? And what of the sacrament often regarded as somehow supplementing or completing baptism: confirmation?

Why does the Church baptize people?

If, as the last chapter suggested, Jesus himself did not baptize many people we have a remarkable historical conundrum. How did it happen that very swiftly after the resurrection, with no apparent discord, his followers adopted baptism as the universal means of entry to his movement?

It is tempting to think the answer is easy: Jesus told them to. Appeal might be made to Matthew 28.16, Mark

16.16 and John 3.5, all of which report Jesus commanding his disciples to baptize. However, this is not wholly persuasive. John 3.5 is at best allusive – if a church only had John's Gospel to go by it might well conclude that what was required was participation in a foot-washing ritual (John 13.8). Matthew 28.16 and Mark 16.16, meanwhile, are acknowledged by the vast majority of scholars to belong to a very late stage in the formation of the gospel record. They are likely to be at least as much reflective of early church practice as generative of it. It is, admittedly, difficult to imagine baptism taking root as easily and universally as it did without some sort of command from Jesus. However, it is equally difficult to see the verses cited, standing alone, as having sufficient force to ground the practice. It would be even more so if we think of Jesus as having rejected the practice of baptism during his ministry: why this confusing volte-face now?

However, Jesus did not reject baptism. He believed that his own ministry was not the time for it, but that is not rejection. Indeed, we have fragmentary evidence that baptism – especially his own – continued to play a significant role in his thinking. It was one of the ways in which he understood the cross looming before him. As John and James dispute who will be greatest in the Kingdom of Heaven, he asks them: 'Are you able to be baptized with the baptism that I am baptized with?' (Mark 10.38 and parallels). Luke's Jesus exclaims, 'I have a baptism with which to be baptized, and what stress I am under until it is completed' (Luke 12.50). Such sayings suggest that Jesus came to see his path, darkening into suffering, as an intensification of the journey begun in the Jordan. His life was a baptism, culminating on the cross.

What, after all, had the Jordan baptism meant? John called people to a baptism of 'repentance for the forgiveness of sins' (Mark 1.4). They were to come out into the wilderness, away from the corruption and complacency of their settled life, to where God had first called the nation into existence. They were to symbolically drown their old lives, be washed and emerge from the waters again – like the wandering Hebrews centuries ago – as God's own people. Such repentance was needed now, urgently, as a sign of readiness for the Mighty One whom John said was coming: the one who baptizes with fire and the Holy Spirit, and would purge the unrepentant wicked from the land.

John's baptism, then, pointed to a great act of God which would forgive the people's sin – which would end their failed, corrupted life and refashion them as the true Israel. To be baptized was to say that one was ready for that, that one wanted to expose oneself to the coming judgement of God. With Jesus, however, things changed. The last chapter suggested that around him, the act of God began to actually happen as Zacchaeus rejoiced and the woman stood up straight. Jesus was the one to whom John's baptism had pointed. Through him, the people would be remade.

Why then was *he* baptized? At one level, it does not make sense – hence John's reported reluctance to do it. Jesus replies that it makes the deepest sense: 'it is proper for us in this way to fulfil all righteousness' (Matthew 3.13–15). It is God's will that the Messiah should undergo the symbolic act of drowning and repentance required of the people. He should act as if all their failure and death is his, go down under the waters with them and for them. He should embrace their death, to bring them to life. This was Jesus' vocation first enacted symbolically in his baptism and then lived out to the uttermost on the cross: to give himself for the forgiveness of sins.

So that Jesus did not baptize in no way marked a rejection of baptism. It was, rather, a significant pause. It marked the fact that what baptism had pointed to was now happening, that the baptism behind all baptisms was right now unfolding. To baptize *now* would be like lighting a candle at dawn. And accordingly, when the early Christians – partly acting on remembered command, partly because Jesus had shared his own sense of baptism with them – began baptizing again, they were not just harking back to John's baptism. The sign was now filled with a different meaning. It no longer just expressed repentance and readiness for the Mighty One. Rather, it was a sign of somehow belonging to, being in the power of, the reality to which John had pointed – Jesus.

The difference between John's baptism and Christian baptism explains those intriguing references in Acts 18.25 and 19.1–5 to Christians who knew only the baptism of John – whom Paul swiftly baptizes in the name of Jesus. Only then (following, significantly, the imposition of Paul's hands – of which more in the final section of this chapter) does Luke tell us the Spirit is given to these believers. John's baptism had anticipated the Mighty One who would pour out the Spirit; Christian baptism was no longer just anticipation but reality – here the Spirit was given.

Paul's most significant comments about baptism come in Romans 6. Here, he refutes those who say that his emphasis upon divine grace as opposed to moral effort encourages laziness: why not go on sinning, so that grace might abound? Paul opposes this vigorously. Christians have died to sin, how can they go on sinning? Paul makes his argument from baptism and assumes that his readers will instantly know what he is talking about:

> Do you not know that all of us who have been baptized into Christ Jesus were baptized into his death? Therefore we have been buried with him by baptism into death, so that just as Christ was raised from the dead by the glory of the Father, so we too might walk in newness of life.
>
> For if we have been united with him in a death like his, we will certainly be united with him in a resurrection like his.
>
> *Romans 6.3–5*

This connection between baptism and death was there in the original symbolism of drowning in the Jordan, and in Jesus' understanding of the cross as a baptism. Now, Paul expects his readers to recognize that in some sense their baptism unites them to the death of Jesus. He seems to be saying that the death of Jesus is no longer just an event 'outside' of the believers, at a specific time and place in external history. It remains that, of course, but through baptism it has also come to be a reality 'inside' believers. His death is something that has happened in them, to them. Paul continues, 'We know that our old self was crucified with him so that the body of sin might be destroyed, and we might no longer be enslaved to sin' (Romans 6.6). Christ's death goes to work in the believers' lives, destroying their old existence of sin. This understanding of the relationship between Christ's death and us, frequently expressed in baptismal terms, is a central Pauline theme.

All this might seem a long way from 'Jesus the joy of God'. However, the two are in fact closely related. God's joy in Jesus, it will be remembered, had as its aim the subversion and defeat of all that stopped Israel and the world from being what God intended: the perfect celebration of the divine life. The name for 'all that stops' this is sin and, as argued in the first chapter, the ultimate expression and consequence of sin is death. Sin runs in each of us individually and together, and individually and together we are locked into death.

In Jesus Christ, God's joy begins to renew all things. Therefore, a great trial between joy and death must come – which is what happens upon the cross. Joy is smothered by death. And the gospel is that joy burns through: that in the end, no power runs deeper and stronger than joy. That next to this, death is nothing at all: 'Where, O death, is your victory? Where, O death, is your sting?' (1 Corinthians 15.55). The cross of Jesus, far from being yet one more place name on the roll call of human defeat, becomes a radiant place. Joy streams from Calvary, victorious, into all misery and begins to raise the dead. All that hammers and nails and violence can do, begins to be undone.

In Paul's mind, to be baptized is to be joined to that place – for the radiant cross to be no longer just without, but within. It is to have a power unleashed within us which destroys the old self – that dominated by sin – and calls the new, joyful, self into existence. In this self the deepest reality is not sin but Jesus, rejoicing. Another way of saying this, which Paul frequently associates with baptism, is to say that the Holy Spirit has been given. For what is the Holy Spirit but the breath of Jesus rejoicing its way into human lives? It begins to raise us from death, and make our whole being joy.

It seems inadequate to introduce the idea of the Church at the very end of this section. In truth, however, it has not been absent thus far. Baptism is understood in the New Testament as the rite of entrance to the Church: that much is boringly obvious. The deeper, more exciting truth is that that is so because the Church is nothing other than the constellation of human lives enlivened by Christ. Where once people were locked away from each other, in fear, competition and hostility, now – transformed by the radiant cross – they are given to each other as gifts. The Spirit turns mutual alienation into joyful friendship in which each may become fully alive.

The Church baptizes people because that is how people become united to the death and resurrection of Jesus. Through baptism, Jesus breathes his Holy Spirit to make his cross and resurrection realities within his followers – sin is burned away, and in its place joy arises. They are made a new people, making each other alive with the fullness of joy. So it is no surprise that even given baptism's all-but-absence from Jesus' ministry the early Church very rapidly decided that it was 'necessary for salvation'.[10]

Is it really necessary?

This begs an obvious question: is sharing in the joy of Jesus really dependent upon being baptized? What about the billions of unbaptized people: are they eternally excluded from joy? That is certainly what much Christian tradition has suggested. The great fourth-century bishop Augustine of Hippo taught that all human beings were born bearing

10 This assertion can be traced from Mark 16.16 and John 3.5 and quickly became unchallenged orthodoxy.

the guilt of Adam's sin, from which they could only be freed by baptism. Even newborn babies, if they died without baptism, would be damned – albeit it only in 'a mild form of damnation (*levissima damnatio*)'.[11] The Church in the West followed his lead for centuries and so it is not surprising that a powerful folk-memory remains to this effect. It is one reason why many who have little to do with the Church still have a strong instinct that their children should be baptized, and why great distress can be caused by any refusal.

The Church today needs to unequivocally reject this aspect of Augustine's theology. God made the world in joy to share his joy, and his all-powerful desire is for the whole creation to rejoice with him. For billions to be condemned to eternal misery would represent the utter failure of the divine purpose – not to mention the problems it would raise in terms of divine goodness. Rejecting Augustine's account, however, does leave us with the difficult question of in what sense baptism can possibly be 'necessary for salvation'. This is a question which must be postponed for now, to be faced squarely in the final chapter.

There is however another sense to the question of baptism's necessity. What has been claimed for baptism is so glorious: how can it possibly be dependent upon the pouring of water? Surely, some might say, if there is any human action which makes one a sharer in Christ's joy it will be faith and obedience, inner dispositions of the heart rather than the performance of a ritual action? The prophets and Jesus agree that God cares far more for the inner reality

11 Augustine, *Contra Julianum*, 5.11.44. For a brilliant, sympathetically critical appreciation of Augustine on this and other matters, see Henry Chadwick, 2009, *Augustine of Hippo: A Life*, Oxford: Oxford University Press, esp. Ch. 11.

of the heart than for external observance. Is the Church's exaltation of baptism (and perhaps of sacraments more generally) not a betrayal of that great spiritual principle? What has ritual got to do with the gospel?

One answer might be to say that in the case of baptism, there is an obvious symbolic connection between the two. This was especially apparent in the baptismal practice of the early Church: with stripping of the candidates, full immersion under the waters, and re-clothing in white robes. All this spoke very clearly of the fundamental spiritual realities of death and rebirth involved – the drowning of an old, sinful nature and the rising to a new, purified life in Christ. Baptism, in short, is a very apt rite for what God intends to communicate through it.

However, something can be apt without being necessary. The Church has always taught (and there are few sentences beginning like that which should not die the death of a thousand qualifications) that baptism is not just a very useful visual aid. Rather, it is the act through which God has commanded the Church to make new Christians. Why should this be the way things have to be? Two fundamental reasons suggest themselves.

First, baptism makes it obvious that Christian life is not fundamentally a matter of what we privately think or feel. It is a very strong temptation (perhaps a form of the classic human temptation to 'be as God') to see *my* decision, *my* action, as the supremely important factor. On such a view, ritual action can only be an expression of and subordinate to human will. The early Church, however, saw matters differently: the primary agent in the sacrament is not us, but God in Jesus. Baptism is not first and foremost our action, but his. The most basic element in Christian life is that before we do anything we are *done to*, caught up in something infinitely greater than and beyond ourselves. The gospel of salvation by grace alone expresses itself most naturally in having the start of Christian life be a ritual we undergo.

Equally, baptism makes it instantly and unmistakeably clear that salvation is a social reality. You cannot baptize yourself: you need another person. There is no private relationship to Jesus apart from the renewed web of lives which is the Church. To belong to Jesus is to belong to that new common life, and thus it makes eminent sense that our sharing in Jesus is mediated through the actions of others in that life. One is not made a Christian in isolation and then invited to join the Church. Rather, Jesus through his Church reaches out to embrace us, and that makes us Christian.

Running through these two reflections – that baptism expresses the primacy of grace and the social nature of salvation – is a common principle: spiritual reality naturally expresses itself in bodily, material, ritual form. These great teachings never remain mere ideas. They are not so much teachings as deeds, enactments of the truth. Baptism communicates its truths by embodying them. Many theologians have referred to this as expressing the 'incarnational principle': that in a religion centred on the Word made flesh, inner spiritual reality normally expresses itself in outer, bodily form.

Therefore, the question 'why should sharing in Christ's joy be made dependent upon the performance of a ritual' should in part be met by asking 'why not?' The question assumes a disjunction between the spiritual and the physical, the inner and the outer, wholly foreign to minds truly shaped by the incarnation. Indeed, the incarnational principle also appeals readily to common sense. Most of us would recognize, for instance, that human love which never expressed itself in bodily form – hugging, kissing, intercourse – would generally speaking be something less than love. The joy of human love calls for enactment, for incarnation in word and gesture and touch. So does divine joy. It brings forth sacraments as naturally as love brings a kiss. Sacraments are God's kisses.

This analogy is also helpful for exploring what kind of sign baptism is. It is, first, a *natural* sign. One doesn't have to explain what a kiss means – unlike, say, the yellow jersey given to the leader of the Tour de France. Kisses, whatever different shades of meaning different contexts lend them, basically express friendship. They also do more than express it: they cement and deepen the relationship. So the kiss is not only a natural but also a *performative* sign. There is a third level of significance, however, which the kiss does not usually quite express. Some signs do more than express or deepen the reality signified: they actually create it. The chess game is not over till the king falls; the peace is not made till hands are shaken. Such signs change reality, and may be called *effective* signs. They do what they signify.

The mainstream view of early Christian tradition, which has endured into contemporary Anglican, Roman Catholic and Orthodox teaching, is that baptism is an effective sign. Something really happens at baptism – people are moved, through the sacrament, from the dominion of death into the new life of joy. If baptism was merely a performative symbol it might plausibly be argued that it should be repeated many times, just as it is good for lovers to kiss many times. All churches are united in forbidding this: what is done in baptism is done once-for-all. You could no more repeat baptism than you could enter in the womb and be conceived again. Spiritually speaking the sacrament is as momentous, decisive and irreversible as the beginning of life itself is. This might be termed a *realist* view of the sacrament, emphasizing the reality of the transformation worked through the sign.

The view may be realist, but is it realistic? Is not the 'effective sign' patently, hideously ineffective? Many of the baptized do not seem at all 'regenerate' – thriving in the joy of Jesus. They appear to slave, like everyone else, under the dominion of sin and death. This objection holds not just against those whose lives are especially scandalous. *All* baptisms are to some degree ineffective: the greatest saints are still sinful and still die. The New Testament and early church history bears some traces of the difficulty which the first Christians, with their great confidence in baptism, had in fully accepting this fact (more of this in the chapter dealing with the sacrament of reconciliation).

So the Church had either to drop the claim that baptism was truly effective, or come to some different understanding of what such language meant. It chose the latter course, and interpreted the claim as being primarily eschatological or future-orientated. The baptized are not *already* perfect, *already* shot through with joy. But this power has been unleashed within them – unstoppably so. However inadequate or catastrophically sinful the baptized are, the deepest fact about them – which even they cannot deny forever – is that they have been made to share in the joy of Jesus. A seed has been planted that will, one day, burst into flower.

At which point we might recall the protest of Paul's imaginary opponent in Romans 6.1: 'What then, shall we continue in sin, that grace may abound?' Is so much emphasis here put on the irresistible power of the renewal effected in baptism, that human agency and freedom are rendered redundant? Does it matter what I do or believe, if baptism itself accomplishes everything – at least in principle? Is nothing required of me?

Concerns like these make many shy away from realist language about the efficacy of baptism, and emphasize instead the personal faith commitment of the candidate or their sponsors. Baptism then is either a divine response to faith, or more radically merely a human action expressing faith. Either way, the prime element in baptism – indeed, in salvation – becomes the human decision of faith. So what at first seems the commendable desire to affirm human responsibility can very quickly undermine the fundamental point of the gospel: that God acts to save us before and apart from any action of ours.

The better response to Paul's opponent should begin instead by rejoicing in the very force of his question: yes, this teaching *does* radically diminish the importance of human agency. An all but irresistible force has been unleashed within the baptized; we may justly doubt whether it is actually possible for them to end in misery. There is an absurdity, an intolerable contradiction about a baptized sinner – and in the end, their identity as baptized will be seen to run deeper and truer than that as sinner. We cannot undo what has been done for us; our freedom is not as decisive as God's love. That is precisely why the gospel is indeed 'good news'.

All that said, there remains another element of truth – that joy is truly 'all but' irresistible. It is the deepest truth of the baptized person's existence, it ever seeks to quicken and enliven us, and it can never be undone. All true, but equally joy will not force. The essence of joy is spontaneity and freedom: so, ultimately, no one can be brought against their will into it. If the baptized person implacably and wholly steers themselves into sin, they can shut themselves out of joy. Whether such self-exclusion could ever be eternal is a different question. Does the joy of Jesus ever reach a 'sell by' date after which its potency is lost? To ask the question is surely to know the answer, even if it would take another book to defend fully.[12] It can never be said with certainty that all will allow themselves to be found, but joy will never stop seeking – and joy is the most creative, resourceful power of all: the very life of God radiating through Jesus. There is every reason to hope that in the end, it will win all things to itself.

Which only raises with sharper force the question postponed earlier: if we may justly hope for all to be saved, who needs baptism or any other sacrament? The answer must wait for the final chapter. For the moment, there is another thorny cluster of issues. *Who* should be baptized? Is it right to baptize babies who presumably have as yet no ability at all to respond to Jesus? Does it matter *whose* babies they are? Should baptism be offered only to infants whose parents are serious about bringing them up in such a way that they will respond to the joy of Jesus? These are some of the toughest practical questions concerning baptism today.

Who should be baptized?

The *Book of Common Prayer* states that 'no minister shall refuse or, save for the purpose of preparing or instructing the parents or guardians or godparents, delay to baptize any infant within his cure . . .' Some ministers, however, interpret the clause about preparation to mean that a high level of Christian commitment must be shown by the parents before their child is baptized. Others ignore it entirely, and

12 Rob Bell, 2010, *Love Wins*, London: HarperCollins, provides one impressive attempt.

baptize infants with virtually no commitment required of the parents. The Church of England thus inflicts its confusion about baptism on the general population, bewildered at the starkly divergent policies of neighbouring churches claiming to share a common life. Christians have perhaps become too comfortable with this mess. It may be politically and practically difficult, but it is a theological, evangelistic and pastoral imperative that the Church as a whole agrees its response to those who seek baptism. That response, I believe, should be a vigorous, theologically confident and unconditional welcome to all who seek baptism. Such a stance is frequently described as one of 'open baptism'.

'Open baptism' has arguably been the default setting of the Church of England and many other 'majority churches' for centuries ('majority' in this context denotes for example the Roman Catholic Church in Ireland, or the Presbyterian in Scotland – where membership of the church has traditionally been closely connected with cultural identity and belonging). To be baptized was part of being a full member of society. Equally, the natural instinct for a ritualized expression of thanksgiving for the birth of a child frequently combined with church teaching on the necessity of baptism for salvation to produce a situation in which baptism simply seemed the 'right' thing to do for infants. While this perception seems to be slackening somewhat now, it remains powerful: around 35 per cent of all babies born in the UK in 2010 were baptized, and all pastors know that to say 'no' to a request for baptism is to risk grave offence.

Churches committed to open baptism rejoice in this happy coincidence of the Church's sacrament with the people's rite of passage for marking birth. Some go so far as to emphasize that baptism *is not* the Church's sacrament: it belongs, rather, to the people who entrust the Church with ministering it on their behalf. These are, after all, Christian people rather than outsiders – in the sense that, at the very least, they have been shaped by culture and history to look to the Christian pattern of story, symbol and ritual to deal with the overwhelming experiences of life and death. The Church should do everything it possibly can to encourage them to keep on using those resources, to inhabit the Christian imagination. That means an enthusiastic 'yes' to requests for baptism, even when people know little of what the Church thinks it means and have even less intent of attending church regularly.[13]

That is not to say that proponents of open baptism have no interest in how people respond to baptism. Some preparation or instruction in the faith may be offered, and such churches would be delighted if this resulted in the candidate and their family being drawn deeper into its life. However, the baptism would not be regarded as a failure if this did not happen. The important thing has already taken place: the child has received the grace of baptism, and the parents' desire for the sacrament has been met by the Church's faithful representation of God's grace, which does not set admission criteria. It is not up to the Church to control what will happen next: God's grace is to be trusted to work in the lives of those touched by the sacrament. Welcome to all, and confidence in God's grace: arguments like these have been for generations the refrain of those committed to open baptism.

Their opponents hold this stance to be missiologically disastrous and theologically wrong. It is missiologically

---

13 The case for open baptism is put powerfully in Alan Billings, 2004, *Secular Lives, Sacred Hearts*, London: SPCK.

disastrous, because it does not call people to the radical change of life which discipleship means. It reduces being a Christian to being a decent, mildly 'spiritual' citizen who nods towards church at Christmas and Easter, wedding and funerals. That clergy should see such nodding as a triumph is evidence that they have failed to understand the call of Jesus. Jesus is to be Lord of every aspect of a Christian's life. Churches should be concerned to promote fully engaged discipleship, which makes real demands – 10 per cent of your income given every month, and not £2 at Christmas time. What is more, if they did so, they would see people respond: there is an appetite for what was once called 'a serious call to a devout and holy life' as opposed to idle religiosity. Churches with open baptism policies, it is frequently claimed, are ageing and emptying; churches with 'tighter' approaches are flourishing as people respond to the challenge.

The missiological disaster of open baptism, opponents argue, is rooted in theological error. Baptism is not a social rite of passage to mark new birth. If it has become such, this process should be urgently reversed. Thankfully, this is in fact happening effortlessly, as fewer and fewer people year by year are using baptism as their new birth ceremony – there is no longer one common rite of passage. This mean baptism's true identity can now be restated: as that which marks the end of an old existence driven by death and the immersion in the new life of Jesus' joy. It can be reclaimed as the sacrament which makes people new, through which Jesus breathes his Spirit into them and their lives are changed once for all.[14]

---

14 The case against open baptism (but in favour of infant baptism) is put very clearly in Colin Buchanan, 1993, *Infant Baptism and the Gospel: The Church of England's Dilemma*, London: Darton, Longman and Todd.

Some critics of open baptism would go further still and urge the Church to revisit the question of whether infants should be baptized at all. If baptism is about the forsaking of an old way of death, and the beginning of a new life in joy, how can it be appropriate for infants? The New Testament teaches that baptism is what should happen to people who come to faith. It is true that propositional belief is neither identical with faith, or even necessarily its most important element. However, those opposed to infant baptism argue faith must at least involve a desire to follow Jesus. The infant has never heard of Jesus: how can she want to follow him? The 'Baptist' conclusion is that we should, therefore, baptize only those able to know what they want. Infants should be welcomed, loved and nurtured towards faith – but baptism must wait.

What response can be offered to these critiques? On infant baptism first: the New Testament is not entirely clear on this question. There is no good reason to suppose that children were excluded from the 'households' which we frequently hear were baptized, and St Paul seems to address children confidently as members of the Body – to which he knows no entry apart from baptism. Certainly the practice of infant baptism grew swiftly and without much apparent discord in the early centuries of the Church. It was not instantly apparent to many before the sixteenth-century Reformation (and only to a minority then) that this was forbidden by Scripture.

Furthermore, the idea that 'only those able to know what they want' should be baptized raises several difficulties. Some disabled people will never be in such a position: are they never to be baptized? And there are less exceptional cases: does an 8-year-old know what they really want? Does a 15-year-old? Does the person beginning to suffer from dementia, or even you reading this? Do we ever have the kind of clarity about ourselves and our desires (let alone those of others) to know with confidence what we or they want? How pure does our intention have to be to 'qualify' for baptism, and who will judge that? Similar problems attend any attempt to require a certain level of intellectual understanding of the faith before baptism. What of those who will never attain such understanding due to mental deficiency? What level of intellectual assent is required anyway: do most adult believers 'understand' what is confessed, for instance, in the Nicene Creed? Who judges what level of understanding is sufficient?

In infant baptism, by contrast, such difficulties do not arise. By definition, it is neither a baby's intellectual understanding nor the quality of their desire to follow Jesus that suits them for baptism. Rather, what matters is that the candidate is beginning a journey of growth in both desire and understanding, indeed in everything which makes up discipleship. What matters is not what has already been attained, but what is being begun. Infant baptism makes sense because the Church, supremely in the parents and godparents, takes responsibility for the infant's lifelong journey into joy. God's grace in baptism is met by the faith not of the tiny child, but of the whole people of God embracing this child as their own. It is important that there is a human response to the joy of Jesus encountered in the sacrament, but for now the infant is, as it were, 'carried' within the response of the whole community.

This immensely attractive view takes its bearings from the basic conviction that baptism is God's work, which is not dependent or conditional upon any human act – the primacy of grace is affirmed. Yet human response is important: grace seeks an answer, seeks to enliven the whole person in the life of Jesus. It is not magic which 'works' utterly regardless of the candidate's agency. However, in stark contrast to strongly individualist accounts (which run counter to the Pauline vision of the body of Christ), this view sees that agency held, nourished and supported from the very beginning by other disciples. This is why, incidentally, godparents have often been considered as of central importance to baptism: because becoming a Christian is about joining the common life.

This defence of infant baptism does not however justify *open* baptism, and many vigorous defenders of infant baptism are scrupulously careful about which infants are in question. The ecumenical statement *Baptism, Eucharist, and Ministry* – to which many churches practising open baptism were (perhaps careless) signatories – warned that '(churches) must guard themselves against the practice of apparently indiscriminate baptism and take more seriously their responsibility for the nurture of baptized children to mature commitment to Christ'.[15] Open baptism was perceived (correctly) as not requiring much evidence of firm intention on anyone's part to ensure that baptized infants were raised as disciples. Accordingly, those who defend infant baptism increasingly do so on the understanding that it is *not* 'indiscriminate', and is offered only to those children whose parents truly intend them to be raised as Christians. In many churches, 'services of thanksgiving and dedication' are now offered to most infants instead of baptism (indeed in some evangelical Anglican churches there seems to be a growing Baptist style reluctance to baptize *anybody's* babies).

There are many reasons to rue all this. The Church might suffer through estranging itself from the folk religion which

15 World Council of Churches, 1982, *Baptism, Eucharist, and Ministry*, 'Baptism', p. 6, para. 16.

still mixes baptism and birth ritual. People will certainly suffer through feeling rejected by the Church, which may become increasingly the preserve of those who are already comfortable within it. To the others, the Church will be yet another institution which implicitly communicates that they somehow do not quite come up to scratch. That may be an unfair interpretation of what is being said, but it will be made. However, can the fundamental theological objection to 'indiscriminate' baptism policies be met? If not, then the pastoral consequences will simply have to be faced.

Remember the theology outlined in the previous section: baptism is the effective sign through which Jesus breathes his Spirit, making his joy the deepest reality of the baptized person's life. This may not be apparent instantly. It may not be apparent at all, throughout the whole life of the candidate. Baptismal grace waits upon the response of the candidate, perhaps until the end of all things. But the unworthiness of the candidate does not hinder the reality of the grace given: our baptized identity as sharers in Christ's joy has become the truest thing about us, whatever we subsequently make of it.

If all this is so, why the great anxiety about whether or not the baptized become practising members of the Church here and now? It is indeed possible, as God respects human freedom, that they may ultimately refuse to enter into the joy of their baptism. It is, however, extraordinarily unlikely. God wills all to be saved; God's love is infinitely potent and resourceful, and has no 'sell by' date. We have every reason to hope that in the end the baptized will become members of 'the Church' – meaning not that they will join our congregations, but that their final destiny is to share in the joy of Jesus.

So far from flying from indiscriminate baptism, the Church should proclaim it as a witness to the indiscriminate grace of God. That grace will seek to awaken human response, certainly. One day, we trust, that response will awaken, in every soul. But grace begins its seeking and enlivening work without reference to our preparedness or checking our credentials – intellectual, moral or parental. Grace rushes to meet us before we have anything to offer: was that not the point of Jesus' story about a prodigal son and his reckless Father? It is worth asking what rigorous baptism policies are trying to defend, since God in Jesus has made it abundantly clear that defence is not among his priorities.

That is not to say that the Church should show no interest in whether baptized infants come to any measure of faith and active discipleship here and now. The Church needs to do all it can to go on mediating the grace which quickens and enlivens human response, all it can to encourage and nurture that response. But it is not ultimately up to the Church to ensure that this happens. People are saved by grace: that is the whole point of the gospel. Ultimately, it is God who in his own time will bring to fruition the seed he planted in baptism.

So, who should be baptized? All who wish, or whose parents wish it for them. Baptism should be gloriously indiscriminate, like grace. Such an approach, however, creates a need for a further decisive ritual or sacrament which marks the moment when the human response to baptism is given freely and maturely, when what the infant is endowed with in baptism is finally claimed by that growing person. That is what the West calls 'confirmation'.

Confirmation

Confirmation once formed – and in the Orthodox world still does – an unbroken unity with baptism. In a sense that unity remains, because confirmation is seen as simply *confirming* what happened in baptism. However, in the most obvious sense – timing – the two sacraments are now very distinct. Most baptisms in the West take place in infancy: confirmation, by contrast, happens in adolescence or later. It has come to mark the time when a person freely identifies themselves with what was done in their baptism, opening themselves to its full power.

The origins of this twofold process of initiation can be seen in Acts 8.15, where we read of Peter and John being sent by the apostles in Jerusalem to the first converts in Samaria, where they prayed that those converts 'might receive the Holy Spirit (for as yet the Holy Spirit had not come upon any of them; they had only been baptized in the name of the Lord Jesus)'. After that startling aside, we read that 'Peter and John laid their hands on them, and they received the Holy Spirit.' Subsequently, in Acts 19.5–6 there is a distinction made between being baptized in the name of Jesus, and receiving the laying on of hands (in this case from Paul) – the latter providing the occasion for the Spirit to be received.

St Luke does not fully explain the relationship between laying on of hands and baptism. These two instances suggest, however, that he saw baptism as at least on occasion properly complemented by the laying on of apostolic hands. The latter action, rather than baptism *tout court*, is seen as effecting the gift of the Spirit to the candidates. St Paul, notably, says nothing of this: but then he is generally uninterested in the detail of ritual or sacramental actions. All his focus is upon the reality conveyed: the new life of the believer in the Spirit.

The precise ritual shape of Christian initiation in the earliest days of the Church is difficult to discern. As has frequently been observed, we have very little evidence to go on. By the third and fourth century, however, it seems that the normal pattern included baptism and laying on of hands (and sharing in communion), administered by the bishop in one service. No one thought in terms of two sacraments, but of one unbroken rite of initiation. However, various pressures soon drove them – in the West at least – apart.

First, there was infant baptism. By the fifth century (and probably for some time before), this was extremely widespread. The sense that baptism effected something of great importance for salvation in the life of the child, combined with very high infant mortality, meant that the demand for infant baptism was overwhelming. Even when bishops were not the somewhat distant figures that they are today for most congregations, it was difficult for them to meet this demand personally. Baptism was thus delegated as a matter of course to the presbyters, and *in extremis* to anyone. However, it was still sensed that identification with the bishop – the symbol of the Church's apostolicity and common life (more of this on the chapter on ordination) – was somehow integral to full Christian belonging. This combined with the pressure for an occasion when the baptized person could freely and maturely claim for themselves what had been done for them in infant baptism. Both factors tended towards the establishment of a second ritual of initiation, celebrated by the bishop, at some distance of time from baptism.

Another pressure was the existence of baptism in communities outside the Catholic Church – in schismatic groups such as the Donatists. This was a movement in fourth- and fifth-century North Africa, larger than the Catholic Church in that region. They existed because of revulsion at the behaviour of certain Catholic bishops in time of persecution, who had willingly handed over holy books to be destroyed by the imperial authorities. Such men, Donatists claimed, were false apostles and the Church they led became false. Real Christians should be outside it, in the Donatists' church – even if that meant they were unrecognized by the rest of the Catholic world. For Catholics, this soon posed the dilemma of what to do if someone baptized by the Donatists then wanted to join the Catholic Church. Had they actually been baptized? Should they be re-baptized? What was the status of Donatist sacraments?

One strict view held that outside the common life generated by and expressed in the sacraments there are no sacraments. Schismatics might do things that look like sacraments, but they have no spiritual reality. One did not 're-baptize' repentant schismatics, but baptized them for the first and only time. Augustine, by contrast, taught that whoever had done the baptizing, the baptism itself was real. The sacrament was effective *ex opere operato* ('on account of the work done'), not *ex opere operantis* ('on account of the one who works'). For Augustine, the human minister is not the most important factor in the communication of grace. The minister may be a scoundrel or a schismatic, but Jesus still gives himself through their actions. As we shall see at various points, this insight became central to western sacramental thought. In Augustine's time, it made reintegration of the Donatists considerably easier, and it underlies the fact that Roman Catholicism today has no difficulty acknowledging the reality of baptisms in communities it regards as schismatic.

However, the obverse of Augustine's generosity must not be forgotten. While schismatic baptism was real, he argued, it could only come to full effect once the candidate lived within the Church. Donatist baptism cried out for completion in full visible belonging to the Church. Laying on of episcopal hands offered an obvious sign of this, and so we arrive at the same destination pointed to by the prevalence of infant baptism: a separate ritual which marks the time when baptism becomes fully effective in the life of the believer, by virtue of that person claiming what was done for them and identifying themselves with the Church in the person of the bishop.

It is especially appropriate that such an occasion be associated with the giving of the Spirit. By coming to the bishop, the candidate expresses their desire to be part of the common life of Christ which takes shape, in part, around that person. As argued in the last chapter, there are no passengers in that common life. Rather, everyone within it is given the responsibility and capacity to bring everyone else to their fullness. The joy of Jesus awakens joy in us, and through us in each other. It makes sense that in the ritual which expresses full membership of that life the Spirit is poured out afresh to enable people to be what they say.

Words like 'full' and 'afresh' beg the obvious question: what happens in confirmation that did not really happen in baptism? What remains outstanding, once someone has been joined through the breathing of Christ's spirit to the heart of his death and resurrection, to share in the joy which streams from it? The clue is in the very word 'confirmation': strengthening, reiteration of what has already been done. Confirmation is therefore radically dependent upon and derivative from baptism. It is why, of all the sacraments treated in this book, confirmation alone does not get a chapter to itself.

An increased recognition of baptism's primacy has caused a radical shift in Church of England practice with regard to confirmation. Once, the norm was that confirmation functioned as a kind of admission ticket to full participation in the eucharist, including reception of communion. Now, many children receive communion before they are confirmed, as is the custom in the Roman Catholic Church. This is much to be lauded. However, the insistence of both churches on a course of preparation, a rite of admission to the eucharist, and a minimum age at which people may receive communion somewhat undermines the point. The Orthodox (and indeed, Augustine's) practice whereby *all* the baptized, infants included, receive communion is much to be preferred. Both options, however, leave the question: what is the point of confirmation now?

Perhaps there is no point. That would be fine: baptism is the one thing needful, not confirmation, and we must not strive too hard to keep a rite alive if it has lost all meaning. However, there are at least three ways in which confirmation might continue to be an important moment in Christian life while no longer the ticket to communion. First, it is the adolescent/adult 'owning' of the faith and of what was said and done to and for one in baptism. Second, it links the individual Christian directly to the bishop – making visible the inner reality of the Church's life as more than just this congregation here and now, as the great communion of saints spread across time and space. Third, as the person takes up their place and ministry in that communion, the Church prays for the Spirit to enable them to play their unique role – to be joy in the way only they can be.

If confirmation is to have such a future, then it must be treated quite differently from baptism. There must be no 'open confirmation' policy, or encouraging all children at a particular stage of education to be confirmed. This sacrament is for those who freely, maturely open themselves to the joy of Jesus playing through them, who respond with all their hearts to what the Spirit breathes in them. A good deal fewer confirmations might be indicative of considerably better spiritual health.

We have already begun to touch on the eucharist. The baptized person is immersed in the death and resurrection of Jesus, their deepest identity is changed forever – reborn – as they go under and emerge from the waters. But that new life, like any infant, needs to be fed and grow and rejoice in belonging. That is what happens in the eucharist, to which we now turn.

FOR DISCUSSION

- Is 'sharing in the death and resurrection of Jesus' part of how you understand being a Christian? What do the words mean to you?
- Quakers and members of the Salvation Army don't practise baptism. Are they Christians?
- How do baptisms in your church express what baptism means? How could they do it better?
- Is there such a thing as a Christian baby?
- Does it matter whether different churches have different baptism policies?

FOR REFLECTION

O font, font, font: this is where my Christian life began.
Michael Ramsey, on visiting the church where he was baptized[16]

We shall not change the old man into a child . . . but we do bring back, in kingly grace, one scarred with sin and grown old in evil habits, to the innocence of a babe.
Gregory of Nyssa[17]

---

16 Cited in Kenneth Stevenson, 1998, *The Mystery of Baptism in the Anglican Tradition*, Norwich: Canterbury Press, p. 96.
17 Gregory of Nyssa, 'On Christian Baptism'.

The Lord indeed says, 'Forbid them not to come to me' (Mark 9.39). 'Let them come', then when they are growing up: let them come if they are learning, if they are being taught where they are coming; let them become Christians when they are able to know Christ.
Tertullian[18]

We yield thee hearty thanks, most merciful Father, that it hath pleased thee to regenerate *this Infant* with thy Holy Spirit, to receive *him* for thine own child by adoption, and to incorporate *him* into thy Holy Church. And we humbly beseech thee to grant that *he* being dead to sin and living unto righteousness, and being buried with Christ in his death, may crucify the old man, and utterly abolish the whole body of sin; and that, as *he* is made partaker of the death of thy Son, *he* may also be partaker of his resurrection; so that finally, with the residue of thy holy Church, *he* may be an inheritor of thine everlasting Kingdom; through Christ our Lord. Amen.
Book of Common Prayer, *Holy Baptism*

'Established Christianity,' whether in the civilized Roman Empire or in half barbarous tribes or in modern nations – the sort of Christianity which claims to embrace the whole society, which it costs men nothing to profess, and into which children are practically baptized as a matter of course – appears to be as audacious a departure from the method of Christ as can well be conceived.
Charles Gore[19]

---

18 Tertullian, *On Baptism*, 18.

19 Charles Gore, 1924, *The Reconstruction of Belief: The Holy Spirit and the Church*, London: John Murray, p. 347.

Holy Baptism (1)

As he that sees a dark and shadie grove,
Stays not, but looks beyond it on the skie;
So when I view my sinnes, mine eyes remove
More backward still, and to that water flie,

Which is above the heav'ns, whose spring and vent
Is in my deare Redeemer's pierced side.
O blessed streams! either ye do prevent
And stop our sinnes from growing thick and wide,

Or else give tears to drown them, as they grow.
In you Redemption measures all my time,
And spreads the plaister equall to the crime.
You taught the Book of Life my name, that so
What ever future sinnes should me miscall,
Your first acquaintance might discredit all.
George Herbert

Almighty and ever-living God,
you have given these your servants new birth
in baptism by water and the Spirit,
and have forgiven them all their sins.
Let your Holy Spirit rest upon them:
the Spirit of wisdom and understanding;
the Spirit of counsel and inward strength;
the Spirit of knowledge and true godliness;
and let their delight be in the fear of the Lord.
Common Worship, *Confirmation*

3

Sharing joy: The eucharist

Eating and drinking with Jesus

If baptism was the hallmark of John's ministry, then feasting seems to have been typical of Jesus: 'Look, a glutton and a drunkard!' (Matthew 11.19). Meals abound in the Gospels, and the symbolic meal of the eucharist remains at the heart of the Church. What Jesus did with food and drink throughout his life offers crucial clues to understanding what, faith trusts, he does with them now.

Perhaps the most obvious meaning of feasting, in Jesus' life as much as our own, is that of joy and delight. According to John, Jesus' first 'sign' was performed at a wedding in Cana (John 2.1–11). There are many meanings to that miracle, but first among them must be the simple expression of God's joy in the joy of his creatures. God created human beings to be a celebration of the divine life; marriage is one of the ways in which humans respond most authentically to that call of our creation (more of this in a later chapter). At Cana, Jesus incarnates the delight of God as his creatures live how they are meant to live. His delight takes the form of ludicrously extravagant quantities of fine wine – the gift of God 'to gladden the human heart' (Psalm 104.15). This was no solemn miracle: this was the giddy raucousness of God, dancing with joy at the joy of bride and groom.

Not a *solemn* miracle then, but still one freighted with meaning. It is no coincidence that it was specifically at a wedding that the divine joy erupted. Jewish hope had long thought of the coming of God to his people, the joining of their life with his, as like a marriage: Ezekiel and Hosea were among those for whom Bride and Groom meant Israel and God. When the messianic era dawned, life would be a great wedding feast. This explains Jesus' answer to those who rebuked his disciples for not fasting: 'the wedding-guests cannot fast while the bridegroom is with them, can they?' (Mark 2.19). The joy of Cana is not just for this man and woman: it heralds the beginning of the great wedding of God and his people (which is why, presumably, John puts it first among Jesus' miracles – it serves as the 'key signature' for all that follows).

This wedding feast has an unexpectedly large guest list. The exuberance of divine joy knows no limits, and calls to its table those who have no right to be there: the failures and the sinners, even those who resist the invitation. That is the message of Jesus' striking table-fellowship with prostitutes and tax collectors. He did not just announce God's embrace of them, but enacted it: his meals became an outward and visible sign of an inward and spiritual grace. Israel was put back together as the joy of God not just in theory but in deed: joy happened.

Food and drink had other resonances in the Jewish imagination upon which Jesus could improvise. Among Israel's founding memories was that of being sustained by manna during the long trek from Egypt to nationhood: in his miraculous feedings in the wilderness Jesus announced that the God of the Exodus was with his people again, perhaps on the move to some still greater act of salvation. This came into sharper focus in the use he made of Passover ritual at the Last Supper. Every year, to re-enact and imaginatively re-experience the events of their liberation from Egypt, the people would slay the Passover lamb and feast on it with unleavened bread and blessed wine. While there is some room for doubt as to whether the Last Supper was actually a Passover meal (the Synoptics suggest so, but John indicates otherwise), it was a meal around Passover time and imbued with Passover significance. Jesus, however, gives it a new meaning, with his enigmatic words over the bread and the wine: 'this is my body, which is for you. Do this in remembrance of me . . . this cup is the new covenant in my blood. Do this, as often as you drink it, in remembrance of me' (so 1 Corinthians 11.23–25, which predates the gospel accounts of the Supper).[20]

Few words have been more mined for meaning, and this book will not plumb all their depths. At the most elementary level, however, what Jesus does here is to associate his own impending death with the Passover sacrifice. What Passover celebrated – God's deliverance of Israel from slavery, its birth as the people of God – Jesus suggests will somehow be brought to a new fulfilment through his Passion. His whole ministry, as we have seen, was about the rebuilding of Israel. Now, his words and actions suggest that all along, the wellspring of this has been sacrifice. All along, Jesus has been giving himself away – into the joy of the wedding at Cana, into the lives of Zacchaeus and the broken woman at the synagogue. He has poured his life

20 The question of the precise words used by Jesus at the Last Supper and their meaning has of course been much debated. See especially Joachim Jeremias, 2011, *The Eucharistic Words of Jesus*, London: SCM Press.

into Israel, and now what this means is to be revealed in its starkest form. At a wedding, where all is happiness and humans are right with God, divine joy is revealed in wine and dancing. But on the night Jesus is betrayed, where joy joins final battle with sin and death – then it must take the form of crucifixion. The joy does not change: it is always the pure playing of the divine life in and through Jesus, but now it meets with no human response save violence. Joy does not fight back, but lets violence do its worst, allows itself to be killed. Only then, with violence all spent, will it be revealed which of the two runs stronger and deeper, which is truly *homoousios* (of one substance) with the deepest reality of all things: God. All that Jesus has done thus far hangs on this contest; only on Easter morning will it be clear whether in the end joy wins.

What happens at the Last Supper is that Jesus reveals the deepest truth of the joy with which he has rebuilt Israel. The redeemed experience it as forgiveness and liberation and abundance, but its essence is Jesus' self-giving. His death was the consummation of this. He emptied himself of all but the divine joy which delights to give itself away into others, and against which in the end violence fails. At the Last Supper Jesus revealed himself as what he always was: the Lamb who takes away the sin of the world, the living sacrifice whose whole being is dedicated to bringing others to joy. The power at work in all Jesus' ministry has been the power of sacrifice.

John's Gospel does not have a record of Jesus' actions with bread and wine at the Last Supper. However, John 6, a sustained meditation on the meaning of Jesus' feeding of the five thousand, encourages us to think along very similar lines to those pursued so far. John's Jesus warns the crowd against simply rejoicing in the fact of a miraculous feeding.

To do so would be to miss the point: 'Do not labour for food which perishes, but for the food which endures to eternal life' (John 6.27). And what is this food? 'I am the bread of life . . . and the bread which I shall give for the life of the world is my flesh' (John 6.48, 51). In other words, the food which will really sustain Israel, which will bring it to the glorious destiny God intends is not physical bread, no matter how wonderfully obtained. It is rather Jesus' life, that great pure act of joy flowing out of itself for the sake of others. If Israel can feed on that, then shall it never die (John 6.50).

Some have said that John's silence about what Jesus said and did at the Last Supper reflects an 'anti-sacramentalism' in his Gospel. On this reading, references to eating the flesh and drinking the blood of Jesus should be understood as a graphic way of describing acceptance of his teachings. At least equally plausible, however, is the suggestion that John 6 (and John 15's meditation on the saying, 'I am the true vine') reflects a very early homily from a celebration of the eucharist. At one point John seems to exult in driving home the sheer carnality of what is involved in feeding on Christ. Strictly translated, John 6.50 reads, 'unless you *munch* the flesh of the Son of Man and drink his blood, you will have no life in you'.[21] You cannot munch an idea: whatever the origins of the saying in either the ministry of Jesus or the mind of John, what is indisputable is that very quickly in early Christian worship these words were understood as

21 Rudolf Bultmann, 1971, *Commentary on the Gospel of John*, Oxford: Blackwell, puts the 'anti-sacramentalism' case; it is well addressed by (among others) Barnabas Lindars, 1972, *New Century Bible Commentary on the Gospel of John*, London: Oliphants, Marshall, Morgan and Scott, pp. 58–9.

meaning that it was through actual physical eating of bread and drinking of wine that Christians fed spiritually on the body and blood of Christ and experienced his joy at work in them.

This would fit very well with the impression in the New Testament that experience of the resurrection was frequently bound up with eating and drinking. Luke's story of two disciples' evening meal with a stranger on the road to Emmaus describes how it was precisely 'in the breaking of the bread' that their eyes were opened, and they suddenly knew the risen Lord (Luke 24.13–35). They had previously heard a report of the empty tomb, but only when the stranger 'took the bread, blessed and broke it, and gave it to them' (v.30) did they experience the truth of resurrection. The way Luke tells their story makes it inconceivable that for him, at least, sharing bread and wine as Jesus had commanded was not a prime way in which Christians could experience his risen power. Equally, for John, Peter's restoration happens in the context of a meal where 'Jesus came and took the bread and gave it to them' (John 21.13). Earlier than Luke or John, Paul asks: 'The cup of blessing that we bless, is it not a sharing in the blood of Christ? The bread that we break, is it not a sharing in the body of Christ?' (1 Corinthians 10.16–17). All these passages suggest that for several strands of New Testament Christianity when the Church did what Jesus had commanded with bread and wine in remembrance of him, it exposed itself anew to his risen power. The joy which had coursed in him in Galilee and Jerusalem coursed now in this act, and made those who shared in it members of his risen body (1 Corinthians 10.17). Through the eucharist, joy was happening once again.

Real presence

All this offers a good way into discussion of a very controversial area in later eucharistic doctrine – namely, the sense in which Jesus is considered to be present in the consecrated bread and wine. This was hotly disputed in the Reformation between Roman Catholicism and various strands of Protestant thought, and one still often hears a contrast being drawn between Catholics who believe that Christ is really, literally present in the bread and Protestants who think instead that the presence is symbolic or metaphorical. The fact that all the terms involved are notoriously slippery does not stop them being thrown around to generate great controversy.

Yet what the first section of this chapter points toward is that, at one level, there is a great consensus on the nature of Jesus' presence at the eucharist. Everyone, from disciples of Thomas Aquinas to those of John Calvin, would agree that in the eucharist Jesus Christ is really present. That is to say, that when the Church does what he commanded with bread and wine it exposes itself to something more than the sum of its own words, actions and thoughts: that rather, here the Church meets the communion-making power of joy, the risen Jesus. On this most central point, there is no great disagreement (save with some radical Protestant Reformers such as Zwingli or Thomas Cranmer).

There has been much dispute, however, on how precisely this real presence of Jesus is related to the bread and wine used. Does Jesus give himself to Christians through the bread and the wine, or does their consumption simply serve as the occasion on which a different, non-carnal communication takes place between the risen Lord and his Church? Is Jesus 'in' these elements to the extent that it is right to venerate them – even to say that they are no longer really bread and wine, but the body and blood of Christ? Or, once the liturgy is ended, are they just ordinary food and drink deserving of no more reverence than my sandwich?

For many centuries, the Church was not over-anxious to answer these questions. The focus was on the more fundamental sense of presence: Jesus making himself the deepest reality of the Church, making his disciples his body. The 'elements' of bread and wine were not treated in isolation from the whole act of which they were part. This is not to say that they were seen as insignificant. Rather, there is uniform testimony across the writings of the Fathers to what can be called a 'sacramental realism': that the bread and wine somehow mediated Jesus, and were to be accorded great reverence on this account. If they were 'symbols' (as many Fathers said), this did not mean that they were mere tokens pointing to a truly absent reality. Rather, they were the means by which Jesus' life was made present. Precisely what this meant for the bread and wine considered in themselves was (largely) left unanswered. What mattered was what they helped make: the Church as the body of Christ. In Henri de Lubac's phrase, it was a matter of 'real presence, because realizing'.[22]

By the second millennium, in the West, this holistic vision had begun to fall apart and there was an increasing focus on the status of the elements in isolation. Why this was so is difficult to discern with precision, but some guesses can be made. Plausibly, as the Church developed through

---

22 'real presence, because realizing' is cited by Catherine Pickstock, 1998, *After Writing: On the Liturgical Cosummation of Philosophy*, New York: Wiley-Blackwell, p. 160. For an excellent survey of early eucharistic doctrine, see J. N. D. Kelly, 1977, *Early Christian Doctrines*, 5th edn, London: A & C Black, Chs 8 and 16.

the centuries it became increasingly difficult for people to imagine that they – dim, sinful, far from Jesus *they* – could really be the body of Christ. As Christendom developed, it was easier (intellectually and morally) to conceive being Christian as a matter of belonging to an institution and attending its rituals, rather than as sharing in the risen life of Jesus. This joined with the ancient intuition that the elements were indeed holy things to create a situation where actual communion at the eucharist became increasingly displaced by treating the rite as a holy spectacle. Something miraculous happened there: the body and blood of Christ appeared as bread and wine. But the miracle was now to be hailed, rather than shared in. The prime sense of the body of Christ was no longer the Church, but the bread made Christ.

There ensued an inflationary spiral, in which the Western Church struggled to give fuller and fuller expression to the dignity of the elements, and the awe in which they were to be held. This, combined with a hunger for formulaic precision in the medieval western mind, abetted by the advent of Aristotelian philosophical rigour in the theology of the twelfth and thirteenth centuries, ultimately gave birth to the doctrine of transubstantiation. Worked out in its fullness by Thomas Aquinas, and defined by the Fourth Lateran Council of 1215, this remains the official Roman Catholic teaching on Jesus' eucharistic presence.

Transubstantiation doctrine relies on a distinction between the 'substance' and the 'accidents' of things. 'Substance' designates what a thing truly is; 'accidents' denote the phenomena through which substance is known. Crucially, substance is *not* physical, despite the word's inevitable connotations to the modern mind. Physical realities belong within the category of 'accidents'; substance speaks of a more basic, immaterial reality.

One helpful illustration is the example of human identity. Our bodies are a process of constant change, decay and renewal. Not one cell endures through our lifetime. Yet *we* endure. The continuity of personal identity must then be located in something which is not physical, yet which constantly generates and co-ordinates our physical existence. This 'something' beyond all accidents is our 'substance'.

According to the doctrine of transubstantiation, at the eucharist God effects a change in the substance of bread and wine with no parallel change in their accidents. To all outward appearance they remain, with exactly the same physical composition and structure as before. It is worth emphasizing this, because both Catholic piety and Protestant polemic have frequently spoken as if some kind of physical change is involved. But the change has happened at the more fundamental, spiritual level of 'substance', where bread and wine are replaced by the body and blood of Christ. At the accidental and utterly unimportant level the appearances of bread and wine remain; what is really and substantially present now is Jesus.

At the Reformation, all this came under sharp criticism from Protestants. For some, the doctrine seemed part of a package in which the Church presumed in some way to repeat the sacrifice of Calvary – the body and the blood of Christ were made present by the priest, and then offered afresh to God for the forgiveness of sins. Not only did this appear to threaten the all-sufficiency of Christ's sacrifice on the cross, it also seemed to give ordained priests almost magical powers and a crucial intermediary role in salvation (we will examine these difficulties in the next section, and in the chapter on ordination). There was also the complaint that transubstantiation was an unscriptural concept, which brought in its wake many equally unscriptural and indeed idolatrous practices. Catholics, Protestant polemic claimed, worshipped bread. Indeed, it requires a determinedly generous cast of mind for a Protestant not to harbour such thoughts when encountering, for example, the practice of Exposition and Benediction with the Blessed Sacrament for the first time.

Protestants proposed various alternatives to the doctrine of transubstantiation, and their arguments among themselves soon rivalled even their disputes with Rome for vehemence. Luther maintained a doctrine of *consubstantiation* – that is, a strong sacramentally realist understanding which held that the two substances (the body of Christ, and the bread) co-existed after consecration. The high reverence for the consecrated elements enjoined by the early Church made sense on this basis, and as in other respects many Lutheran churches maintained considerable continuity with Roman Catholicism. Calvin, by contrast, ultimately severs the presence from the elements themselves. Their consumption is used by God, certainly, as a prime occasion on which the Spirit unites believers to the risen Jesus. But there is no hint of confusion or identity between bread and wine and Jesus. The elements are God's tools, not his body.

The Anglican position was difficult to pin down. Famously, the English mode of reformation was reluctant to be overly doctrinaire, and there were certainly a range of viewpoints within the reformed English church with only transubstantiation ruled firmly excluded by Article 28 of the 39 Articles. Calvin certainly exercised great influence over sixteenth-century English Reformers and their eucharistic doctrine. However, there was a gradual parting of the ways between Anglicanism and the Calvinist tradition, with Anglicanism eventually looking rather more Lutheran in this respect.

One scholar has described the Anglican position as characterized by a 'Reformed Patristic' approach.[23] It is Patristic insofar as it shares both the sacramental realism of most Fathers and their reluctance to state too precisely exactly what this means for the elements; it is Reformed in rejecting transubstantiation and associated beliefs and practices, and in reorienting the purpose of the eucharistic presence towards communion.

Why prefer any of these doctrines to another? Remember that on the one thing needful – the real, active presence of Jesus feeding the Church with himself, making it his body – there is no real dispute. The question of what exactly this means for the elements is not unimportant, but must be set within the context of this bigger, deeper consensus. That said, there are good reasons for pursuing one of the 'sacramentally realist' options – that is, the characteristically Anglican, Lutheran, Roman Catholic and Orthodox views which see the consecrated bread and wine as mysteriously more than themselves, as bearing Jesus and so deserving great reverence. First, this is the overwhelming impression left to us by the testimony of the Fathers. This is how the first Christian centuries understood the sacraments and Scriptures; we need a strongly pressing reason before setting it aside. We should be sufficiently Reformed to acknowledge the theoretical possibility of such a reason, and sufficiently Catholic to be deeply sceptical of each candidate advanced.

Sacramental realism has more to commend it than tradition, however. It is deeply consonant with the way

23 Kenneth Stevenson, 1994, *Covenant of Grace Renewed: A Vision of the Eucharist in the Seventeenth Century*, London: Darton, Longman and Todd, p. 185.

Christianity believes God works in the world, supremely in the incarnation. God uses created reality – ultimately, the human nature of Jesus – as the vehicle of his presence in the world. That humanity is not a mere visual aid or temporary instrument, but the enduring way in which God enters into the world. Equally, according to shared Christian orthodoxy as expressed in the creeds, our own bodies and human nature are not to be cast aside but to become the stuff of divine joy. Why, in the eucharist, should God work in a different way than in the incarnation from which sacraments spring and in the glory towards which they point? Created, physical reality shone and will shine with the glory of God: why not bread and wine?

A further consideration suggests itself. The last chapter argued that one of the reasons Christian life begins with baptism is to make clear from the beginning that salvation is a matter of being done to, and of being done to *together*. A similar rationale may be at work here. If – as on Calvin's scheme – being united to Jesus is ultimately separable from, independent of the eucharistic elements, then it is all too easy for such union to be reduced to a private, internal communication between the soul and God. That then equally easily degenerates into a matter of my feelings, my religious experience, my struggling to make God real in my mind. Sacramental realism, by contrast, makes it unmistakeably clear that my union with Christ happens because he comes to me, and he comes to me only as I share his meal with others, only as I am part of his body.

There is much to be said then for sacramental realism. What, though, of transubstantiation? Does it say anything more? The First Anglican–Roman Catholic International Commission (ARCIC-1) judged not, and proclaimed an agreed eucharistic doctrine in sacramentally realist terms without using the terminology of transubstantiation. This was not because, it noted, anything such language claimed was to be denied but because it was not clear what would be added by using it. It seemed that the matter, for so long controversial in Anglican–Roman Catholic relations, had been resolved with unexpected ease.[24]

However, things are seldom that simple. The Vatican refused to allow that ARCIC-1 had reached genuine consensus between the two traditions.[25] To understand why, we should turn to the 1994 *Catechism of the Catholic Church*, which illustrates its teaching on transubstantiation with a quotation from a hymn attributed to Aquinas. Speaking of the consecrated elements, it says: 'Seeing, touching, tasting are in thee deceived.'[26] They are deceived because in some sense, for Roman Catholic teaching the most important sense, the bread and wine are no longer there. Their 'accidents' may remain, but at the most profound level the natural elements have been abolished and replaced by the body and blood of Christ. ARCIC-1 did not speak in such terms, suggesting that one could speak of the real presence of Christ being given in and through bread and wine without in any way diminishing or abolishing the latter. Sacramental realism will certainly affirm that the consecrated elements are *more* than mere bread and wine; transubstantiation doctrine makes a further problematic step by saying that they are in some sense *less*.

---

24 See *Anglican–Roman Catholic International Commission: The Final Report, Windsor, September 1981*, 1982, London: CTS/SPCK.

25 'The Official Roman Catholic Response to the Final Report of ARCIC-1', in Christopher Hill and Edward Yarnold, eds, 1994, *Anglicans and Roman Catholics: The Search for Unity*, London: SPCK, pp. 156–66, para. 22.

26 *Catechism of the Catholic Church: Popular and Definitive Edition*, 2000, London: Burns and Oates, p. 311, para. 1381.

At this point some readers may be tempted to despair of theological subtleties and wonder whether such a refined debate can possibly matter. The temptation is understandable, but in fact this dispute touches on a question at the heart of sacramental theology and indeed of Christianity: does God work with and through created realities, or does he ultimately dispense with them? The doctrinal history of the first Christian centuries, above all the history of the doctrine of the incarnation, is the story of a clear answer to that question emerging through hard and repeated struggle. First, it was established that Jesus Christ had a real human body; next that he had a real human mind and soul; next that his human nature was like ours in all things except sin (that is, except in that which deforms our human nature); next, that this meant that he must indeed have had a truly human will. Jesus is certainly more than a mere man, but he is equally certainly in no way less.[27] Ironically, it was Thomas Aquinas who gave the principle its classic formulation: *gratia non tollit naturam sed perfectit* – 'grace does not abolish nature, but perfects it'. Thomas' transubstantiation doctrine seems to belie his own best instincts.

So these differences really matter. However, their importance can be overstated. Whatever the magisterium might teach, experience suggests that when most Roman Catholics use the language of transubstantiation what they are really contending for is the sense that the eucharistic elements are 'not just bread', 'not just wine'. Something more than symbol or metaphor (or at any rate than the impoverished meanings often attached to those words) is encountered here: the

27 The story is told with exceptional clarity in Stephen W. Need, 2008, *Truly Divine and Truly Human: The Story of Christ and the Seven Ecumenical Councils*, London: SPCK.

real presence of Jesus is being given in, with and through bread and wine. Pressed much more than that, the doctrine begins to creak ominously. But insofar as it tries to make that basic point there is not much disagreement between Roman Catholics, Anglicans and many others. Might the same be true in another highly controversial area, that of eucharistic sacrifice?

Eucharistic sacrifice

The *Book of Common Prayer* leaves one in little doubt that something is being ruled out very emphatically indeed in its service of Holy Communion. The prayer of consecration speaks of Christ making 'by his one oblation of himself, once offered, a full, perfect, and sufficient sacrifice, oblation and satisfaction for the sins of the whole world'. Whatever the Church does now in the eucharist it is most definitely not, according to the BCP, repeating, renewing or supplementing what Jesus did on the cross. The only sacrifice we offer in the eucharist is that of 'thanks and praise': wholly different from, dependent upon and responsive to Jesus' sacrifice on the cross.

The Prayer Book here expresses an allergic reaction, common to all early Protestant theology, against perceived Roman Catholic doctrine. Allegedly, Roman Catholics believed that the point of transubstantiation was to allow the priest to re-offer to God Christ's body and blood. This sacrifice was offered on behalf of the living and the dead, and won for them the forgiveness of sins. As the sixteenth-century Council of Trent (which vigorously re-asserted Catholic teaching against Reformation critiques) stated: 'the victim is one and the same: the same now offers through the ministry of priests, who then offered himself on the cross; only the manner of offering is different . . . (and since) the same Christ who offered himself once in a bloody manner on the altar of the cross is contained and is offered in an unbloody manner (in the eucharist) . . . this sacrifice is truly propitiatory.'[28] Today, in Roman Catholic liturgy, the eucharistic prayer is preceded by the congregation speaking to the priest: 'May the Lord accept this sacrifice at your hands, for the praise and glory of his name, for our good, and the good of all his church.' Many Protestants still find such language surprising and difficult to accept.

There were, and are, many reasons for this. Some dislike the language of sacrifice altogether, because it seems distastefully redolent of primitive religions anxious to appease their angry gods through violence and killing. For others the imagery has died through its political exploitation by leaders keen to have others offer 'the supreme sacrifice' in war. The classic Protestant reaction has different motivations. Protestants, often quite relaxed about seeing Jesus' death as a bloody sacrifice to appease God, rejected instead the perceived suggestion in Roman Catholic teaching that somehow this sacrifice needed renewal or even repetition by the actions of the Church or its ordained priesthood. The latter, they feared, came to be seen not only as endowed with quasi-magical power to effect transubstantiation, but as in some sense a sacrificing intermediary between the people and God, reminiscent of Jewish or pagan priesthoods. Protestant Reformers argued that the New Testament and Patristic emphasis upon every Christian sharing the life of the risen Jesus through communion had been effectively

28 *Catechism of the Catholic Church*, p. 307, para. 1367.

replaced by Rome with a new cult of sacrificial spectacle, to be watched from afar by the laity. This cult combined with the doctrine of Purgatory to create opportunity for both superstition and exploitation, as people paid money for priests to offer sacrifice in order to help loved ones towards heavenly bliss. Which brings us, finally, to the most fundamental criticism: Luther's central conviction, and the heart of all Protestant theology, is that human beings are saved by grace alone and contribute nothing to their salvation. The Roman Catholic doctrine of the mass, however, seemed to say that there was something human beings could do, indeed must do, to earn salvation for themselves and for others: namely, offer the eucharistic sacrifice.

Protestants tried to expunge all this from their eucharistic doctrine and practice. References to sacrifice disappeared from their liturgies, or were so handled as to rigorously exclude any hint of the Roman doctrine. Priests lost their special vestments, and in most Protestant churches lost even the name 'priest'. They were to be seen not as magicians and sacrificers, but as the teachers and leaders of the Church: presbyters, not priests. Altars became communion tables: no longer placed so as to be gazed at by the laity from afar, but so that all could share in the Lord's Supper remembered there. The dead too all but disappeared from the liturgy, in what Eamon Duffy has called 'an act of exorcism, (limiting) the claims of the past, and the people of the past, on the people of the present'.[29] Nor has all this abated: in the early twenty-first century the Church of England studiously avoided using the verb 'to offer' or

29 Eamon Duffy, 1992, *The Stripping of the Altars: Traditional Religion in England 1400–1580*, New Haven and London: Yale University Press, p. 8.

its cognates in connection with bread and wine in its new eucharistic prayers, preferring instead to speak of the Church either 'bringing' or 'setting before' God. Such hair-splitting is almost comical, but has miserable roots in deep aversion to the Roman Catholic doctrine of eucharistic sacrifice.

Why 'tragic'? Because whatever the justification for Protestant reaction against the late medieval understanding of eucharistic sacrifice, much was lost because of it – which could have been saved by a more charitable interpretation of what Roman Catholicism actually taught, and by returning to earlier traditions. While this perhaps has not always been unambiguously obvious, Roman Catholicism has never really meant to say that the sacrifice of Calvary is any way repeated or supplemented in the mass. The two historical events – the death of Jesus and each eucharistic celebration – are never, as it were, put on the same level, made the same kind of event. Rather, the celebration of mass is seen as an act by which the once-for-all sacrifice of Calvary is made present.

That is an easy sentence to write, but a difficult idea to absorb. One clue to understanding might be to remember Paul's teaching about baptism in Romans 6.3–5, where he presents the death and resurrection of Jesus as being mysteriously more than events locked in the past, 'outside' the lives of believers. They remain real historical events of course (just as bread remains bread, perhaps?) but simultaneously are more than historical events. They are not *over*, but have made themselves the deepest reality of all time and of the believers' lives. This is why one of the most dismal moments in contemporary liturgy is when we describe the eucharist as a 'memorial' of the death and resurrection of Jesus. The word evokes tombstones and cenotaphs, and is utterly inadequate to convey what the Fathers meant by 'remembrance'. For them, the eucharist was not a memorial service but the act in which Jesus Christ surged into the life of believers and seized them with his joy. Remembrance is not about fondly recalling Jesus, but about being seized by the power of his death and resurrection.

Which means, of course – recalling the first section of this chapter – being seized by his sacrifice. Remember what Jesus signified at the Last Supper: that the deepest energy at the heart of his ministry was his pouring himself out so that others might live. That is joy: the great self-sharing which makes others come alive. Jesus is always, and supremely on the cross, the one in whom there is nothing but love pouring into the loveless, that they might lovely be. That is what his sacrifice really means. For his followers, to receive communion is be brought within the power of this sacrifice. Indeed, it is to be changed into this sacrifice – to have one's own life filled with the joy of Jesus, to be made progressively like him, in the end to be nothing but love: 'it is no longer I who live, but it is Christ who lives in me' (Galatians 2.20). That is why after communion we pray, 'and now we offer you, Lord, our souls and bodies, to be a living sacrifice'. Neither the eucharistic sacrifice, nor the presence, is something outside of believers to be gazed on from afar. Rather, Jesus is present as sacrifice drawing us into himself. We are immersed ever more deeply in his joy, become ever more deeply his joy. The great paschal moment is not repeated, any more than baptism – but we are plunged ever further into it, so it may run ever more freely in us.

There is little emphasis here upon the offering of the bread and wine themselves. That is because they have their (great) importance not considered in isolation but precisely insofar as they are the media through which Jesus feeds his people with himself. The prime focus is not on them being sacrificed but on how we, through them, are made sacrificial. That important point established, however, there is *a* sense in which it is worthwhile to speak of 'sacrificing' the elements. At one level, bread and wine represent the resources of life and all created goods. Left to our own devices, human beings hoard these. Ownership and distribution of goods become one of the ways in which communion between people is destroyed. The joy of Jesus meets this tendency and begins to dissolve it, begins to make us treat bread and wine and all other created goods no longer as tokens of wealth and power, but as means of sharing. In one sense, people who share in the joy of Jesus do not own things: rather everything about them is to become part of the great self-sharing that he is. Relinquishing, sacrificing our goods is a genuine part of the eucharist (another reason, incidentally, why it is important to maintain the true 'bread and wine-ness' of the elements. As Rowan Williams has put it, their eucharistic use now 'shadows' their secular use, and calls it into question.[30])

If the joy of Jesus dissolves the way in which we carve each other up socially and economically, it does so no less with the great barrier of death. In the first chapter, we saw that this was the great enemy to be defeated: the ultimate power working against communion. Death drives us apart from each other and apart from God, it is the great mockery of all joy's purpose. That was why Jesus' mission of joy required the great confrontation with death on Calvary and in the tomb. The essence of the gospel is that there was begun the undoing of death, that the joy which knits things together in love ultimately runs stronger and deeper than that which divides and

30 Rowan Williams, 2000, 'The Nature of a Sacrament', in *On Christian Theology*, Oxford: Blackwell, pp. 197–208, p. 207.

kills. The dead are reclaimed for the human family – a fact given graphic expression in the tradition of eastern iconography where Jesus is seen as hauling Adam and Eve out of hell.

The risen life of Jesus which surges towards and within us in the eucharist is a life which brings with it our dead. It makes good sense, then, to name them in our liturgies. We are in communion with them, just as much as with those with whom we gather in church. This was the deeply healthy instinct which lay in the ancient custom of prayers for the dead in the course of the eucharist. It does not remotely compromise the truth that salvation is by grace alone, any more than praying for anyone does. Rather (as when praying for anyone), what we do is express grateful confidence that the dead remain enveloped in the joy of Jesus, working its transfiguring grace on them as on us.

There is, however, a still more striking truth. The Reformers were surely right to criticize the system whereby it looked like the Church did something for the dead through eucharistic sacrifice in a rather mechanistic fashion: the priest performs the ritual, and God discounts a certain period of 'time' from the ancestor's stay in Purgatory. It is not so easy to mock the idea, however, that in a certain sense the dead wait for us. That is to say, joy's purposes will only be accomplished when the whole human family (the whole creation?) is joined together in joy. We are part of one life, members of one body: no one's destiny can be fully realized without everyone else's. The dead yearn for us to know joy, in part because their own joy demands it. They shall not be perfect without us (Hebrews 11.40).

That means, simply, that it *matters* to the dead when we celebrate the eucharist and receive communion. Not only do we 're-member' them, celebrating Jesus' reclamation of them for the human family from the nothingness of death, but we also bring them closer to the fullness of joy. We do that by being drawn ourselves ever more deeply into the one life of joy which all were created to celebrate together. Astounding as it sounds, the apostles Peter and Paul in some sense wait for us to know the fullness of Christ's joy because until we do, they cannot. And so the act by which we are brought more deeply into that joy brings them along too. The joyful sacrifice which envelops us in communion, envelops them. If we think about it this way, it is absolutely correct to describe the eucharist as 'a sacrifice for the living and the dead'. To do so does not deny the gospel so much as announce its greatest promise: that we all belong together, in the joy of Jesus.

But if that is so – if the eucharist is all about the ending of divisions – why do Christians not celebrate it together?

Unity

It hurts to be turned away by other Christians from sharing in communion. Whatever the rationale offered, it feels like an insinuation that in some sense the rejected ones are not 'real' Christians. It seems too a staggering reversal of the hospitality of Jesus, who welcomed sinners as well as the righteous. For many years now, Protestants have been accustomed to sharing the eucharist in each other's churches (though it was not always thus, and there still remains occasional reluctance to see each other's sacramental ministry as being fully real). So the refusal of both the Orthodox and Roman Catholic Churches to countenance 'inter-communion' with Protestants is greeted with hurt incomprehension shading into resentment.

A defence of the Roman Catholic and Orthodox position might begin by noting that despite the best efforts of ecumenists or of this chapter, there remain deep gulfs in eucharistic theology between the churches. The previous section noted the outstanding difficulties around the doctrine of transubstantiation. More fundamentally, however, many Protestant Christians (including many Anglicans) would dissent sharply from the ideas of eucharistic presence and sacrifice set out above. Judged from the standpoint of the Vatican, we may not have said quite enough; judged, for instance, from the standpoint of the strongly Protestant Anglican Diocese of Sydney we have said far too much. So even before the ordination of women, the most recent 'spanner in the works' obstructing unity from the official Roman Catholic and Orthodox perspective (unsurprisingly, to be explored in a subsequent chapter), it could justly be asked: do Protestant churches know what they think about the eucharist? And if they do, is it anything like what Rome and the Orthodox think? Negative answers to either question might be thought to justify the continued refusal to share communion.

An honest assessment would have to hold that there are indeed many opinions among Protestants about the eucharist (as indeed, there are among Roman Catholics and Orthodox Christians). It would also admit that many of these opinions (even among Anglicans, despite ARCIC's wishful thinking) are strongly opposed to the teachings of Roman Catholicism and Orthodoxy. However, if common doctrine is what matters, we should not forget the strong and broad consensus which holds that in the eucharist, Jesus feeds us with himself and brings us into his risen life. Arguably that is the one thing needful, and the rest – presence, sacrifice, priesthood – is not unimportant, but secondary. After all, the Orthodox firmly reject transubstantiation and that doesn't stop eucharistic sharing with

Rome. Why should doctrinal differences with Protestants matter more?

Difference of doctrinal detail, however, is not at the heart of the Roman and Orthodox refusal of inter-communion with Protestants. That lies rather in the conviction that communion is the outward and visible sign of an inward and spiritual reality – shared life in Jesus. At present that shared life is deeply broken. There is insufficient real communion between the churches for us to enact communion in eucharistic sharing. There is a rather exact analogy with the traditional Christian teaching that sexual intercourse belongs exclusively within marriage. Intercourse has been considered as the outward and visible sign of an inward and spiritual love. Man and woman fused at the deepest levels of their being in love naturally express this union through their bodies. Bodily union in the absence of such deep spiritual fusion is a kind of lie: the outward and visible sign without the inward and spiritual reality. For Rome and the Orthodox, the same would be true of eucharistic sharing between divided churches. It is better to wait until the partners are truly one before physically celebrating the fact.

There are at least two problems with this line of argument. First, the analogy with marriage cuts both ways. To anticipate a later chapter, experience suggests that frequently sex comes well before the full flowering of marriage. When it does, it is not always telling a lie (this is one occasion where it is not irrelevant to observe that official Roman Catholic and Orthodox doctrine is, by and large, made by celibates). Rather, sex has been found by many couples to be a way into deeper love: food for the journey, rather than simply its triumphant conclusion. It is sometimes argued that were eucharistic sharing to happen before full unity is accomplished, it might somehow dull the desire for that unity. The history of intercommunion between Protestant churches shows that that concern is not wholly misplaced, but the analogy with sexual experience tells us that it can work the other way too. It is worth noting too that few things have been more effective in dampening the ardour for unity with Rome and the Orthodox among Protestants than the long refusal of communion.

Moreover, Roman Catholicism and Orthodoxy are divided among themselves. Full unity would mean a common life, with wholly shared patterns of ministry and authority – quite simply being one Church. They are not, and yet they share communion. As the Catholic *Catechism* puts it, 'a certain communion *in sacris*, and so in the eucharist . . . is not merely possible but is encouraged'. This might seem inconsistent, but Rome gives a very clear reason why the cases are quite different. Of the Orthodox, it states: 'These Churches, though separated from us, yet possess true sacraments, above all – by apostolic succession – the priesthood and the Eucharist.' By contrast, 'Ecclesial communities derived from the Reformation and separated from the Catholic Church have not preserved the proper reality of the eucharistic mystery in its fullness, especially because of the absence of the sacrament of Holy Orders.'[31]

In other words, a Roman Catholic can share communion with the Orthodox because their eucharist is really the eucharist. This is because the Orthodox have preserved the apostolic succession: their bishops and priests stand in an unbroken line of appointment from the apostles (more on the significance of this claim in the chapter on ordination). According to Roman Catholic doctrine, Protestants – even

31 *Catechism of the Catholic Church*, p. 316; paras 1399–400.

Anglicans who fondly imagine otherwise – have not maintained this succession. Their clergy may be excellent teachers and pastors, but they are not real apostolic bishops and priests. Whatever they do with bread and wine – and it is of some real, if unspecified, value) – it is not the eucharist (*Catechism*, para. 1400). Indeed, speaking with utmost precision they are not churches, but 'ecclesial communities'.[32] The real Church is that which possesses unbroken continuity of ordination with the Twelve, and ultimately with Jesus Christ.

A fully adequate response to this would go well beyond the confines of this chapter and even this book. For now, it must suffice simply to sketch how such a response might go. It could begin challenging on purely historical grounds the claim that any church possesses an unbroken chain of continuity with the apostles. Quite simply, we know too little about the development of ordained ministry in the first few decades and centuries to affirm this with any confidence. Secondly, it could claim that the history of the Church and its ordained ministry is so morally and spiritually ambiguous that institutional continuity can be easily overrated. In what sense other than the purely legal was a Borgia a successor of the apostles? To make being the Church utterly dependent on such succession seems extravagant (though we should equally avoid the opposite error of disregarding it entirely – more of this later).

There should also be a theological challenge to the Roman position. One does not have to be radically dismissive of the place of institutional continuity in the life of the Church

32 This claim is developed in 'Sacred Congregation for the Doctrine of the Faith', 2000, in *Dominus Iesus: On the Unicity and Salvific Universality of Jesus Christ and the Church*, London: Incorporated Catholic Truth Society.

to wonder if God cannot work beyond and without it. Even if Roman Catholicism and Orthodoxy had the apostolic ministry they presume to, even if this ministry had a better record than it does, and even if it were granted that all Protestants have abandoned it – why would it follow that a Protestant eucharist was not 'the real thing'? Succession in the ministry is not the *only* thing that makes the Church one across space and time: we should rather see such succession as one outward and visible sign (among others: shared sacraments, creeds, Scriptures) of a unity which is truly inward and spiritual – our sharing in the joy of Jesus. Apostolic succession in the ordained ministry might sustain and express that more fundamental reality; one might even say that it is, all things being equal, its natural sign. But the reality creates the sign, not the other way around. A church's eucharist is real not because its clergy have a certain institutional pedigree, but because the joy of Jesus wells up through all the community is. And that joy welcomes all Christians to its table.[33]

Or does it? For much of Christian history it has rather been assumed that certain kinds of sin bar one from sharing in communion. In Roman Catholic theology another sacrament is then of vital necessity: that of reconciliation, frequently known as confession. Another sacrament, another occasion of fierce controversy between the traditions. We turn now to this sacrament along with its twin, the anointing of the sick: joy's ways of grappling with the great enemies, sin and death.

---

33 Space prohibits discussion here of a question increasingly being raised by the 'open table' movement in the United States: if joy truly welcomes all, should not the unbaptized be welcomed to communion?

FOR DISCUSSION

- How frequently should Christians celebrate the eucharist?
- What – if anything – should be required of people before they share communion? Does it matter what they believe, or how they behave?
- What happens with the bread and wine in your church after communion, and what does this say about beliefs concerning them?
- How helpful is 'sacrifice' as a way of thinking about the eucharist?
- 'Avoid stupid controversies, genealogies, dissensions, and quarrels about the law, for they are unprofitable and worthless' (Titus 3.9). Which disputes concerning the eucharist are 'stupid'?

FOR REFLECTION

Just as the bread, which comes from the earth, when it receives the invocation of God, is no longer common bread but eucharist, being composed of two elements, a terrestrial one and a celestial, so our bodies are no longer commonplace when they receive the eucharist, since they have the hope of resurrection to eternity.
Irenaeus of Lyons[34]

The ultimate change intended by God is the transformation of human beings into the likeness of Christ. The bread and the wine *become* the sacramental body and blood of Christ in order that the Christian community

34 Irenaeus, *Adversus Haereses*, 4:18,5.

may *become* more truly what it already is, the body of Christ.
First Anglican–Roman Catholic International Commission[35]

. . . the flesh of Christ is like a rich and inexhaustible fountain, which transfuses into us the life flowing forth from the Godhead into itself. Now, who sees not that the communion of the flesh and blood of Christ is necessary to all who aspire to the heavenly life?
John Calvin[36]

Your mystery is laid on the Lord's table, your mystery you receive. To that which you are, you answer 'Amen', and in answering you assent. For you hear the words 'The Body of Christ' and you answer 'Amen'. Be a member of the Body of Christ, that the Amen may be true.
Augustine[37]

. . . through fellowship in the perfect sacrifice of the Son of Man, we ourselves become that sacrifice.
Charles Gore[38]

The command, after all, was *Take, eat*: not *Take, understand*. Particularly, I hope I need not be tormented by the question 'What is this' – this wafer, this sip of wine.

---

35 ARCIC-1, 1982, p. 21.

36 John Calvin, 1989, 1559, *Institutes of the Christian Religion*, tr. Henry Beveridge, Grand Rapids, Michigan: Eerdmans, Book IV, Ch. XVII, 9, p. 563.

37 Sermon 272.

38 Charles Gore, 1901, *The Body of Christ: An Enquiry into the Institution and Doctrine of Holy Communion*, London: John Murray, p. 286.

That has a dreadful effect on me. It invites me to take 'this' out of its holy context and regard it as an object among objects, indeed as part of nature. It is like taking a red coal out of the fire to examine it: it becomes a dead coal.
C. S. Lewis[39]

Don't let (your sins) be an excuse for not communicating. You can go with a sure trust in Him Whom you will there receive. You do not bring down his divine greatness to your own littleness. He lifts you up into Himself.
Gregory Dix[40]

. . . the new tendency is to emphasize that holy communion is 'corporate'. We are urged to speak of 'our communion' and to suspect the phrase 'my communion'. Certainly a truth is here being recovered. But holy communion involves nonetheless the responsible act of an individual, and it is an act full of awe and dread . . . the awe in the individual's approach to holy communion, which characterized both the Tractarians and the Evangelicals of old, stands in contrast to the ease with which our congregations come tripping to the altar week by week.
Michael Ramsey[41]

---

39 C. S. Lewis, 1964, *Letters to Malcolm: Chiefly on Prayer*, London: Geoffrey Bles, p. 107.

40 Cited in Simon Jones, 2007, *The Sacramental Life: Gregory Dix and his Writings*, Norwich: Canterbury Press, p. 53.

41 Michael Ramsey, 1956, 'The Parish Communion', in *Durham Essays and Addresses*, London: SPCK, pp. 15–21, 19.

Accept through him, our great high priest,
this our sacrifice of thanks and praise,
and as we eat and drink these holy gifts
in the presence of your divine majesty,
renew us by your Spirit,
inspire us with your love
and unite us in the body of your Son,
Jesus Christ our Lord.
Common Worship, *Eucharistic Prayer A*

4

Joy heals (I): Reconciliation

One important theme encountered in this book so far has been the theme of sacramental realism. This means, for instance, that the bread and wine of the eucharist are somehow 'more than' mere bread and wine, and bear with them the body and blood of Christ. It means also that through the sacraments, joy is really happening to us. These signs effect what they signify: in the waters of baptism we are plunged into the death and resurrection of Jesus, which goes to work within us to destroy sin and bring glory. In the eucharist, Christ continues to surge towards and within us, deepening our communion of joy with his whole body. Through the sacraments, joy floods in and we are changed.

Except of course that we are not – at any rate, not as radically, obviously and enduringly as this sort of language suggests. Baptized Christians who share communion sin, sometimes appallingly. It was initially very difficult for the Church to acknowledge or theorize this fact, which is why the author of 1 John can write: 'No one who abides in [Christ] sins; no one who sins has either seen him or known him . . . Those who have been born of God do not sin, because God's seed abides in; they cannot sin, because they have been born of God' (1 John 3.6, 9). Being 'born of

God', of course, was precisely what Johannine Christianity thought happened to people in baptism. Yet alongside such uncompromising statements, 1 John has more realistic moments: 'If we say that we have no sin, we deceive ourselves, and the truth is not in us. If we confess our sins, he who is faithful and just will forgive us our sins and cleanse us from all unrighteousness' (1 John 1.8–9). The enduring facts of sin and forgiveness in the Christian life imply the subject matter of this chapter: the sacrament of reconciliation, sometimes also known as that of confession or penance. This chapter will use the term 'reconciliation' to indicate all that has traditionally been seen as belonging to this sacrament: the believer's repentance, their confession, the absolution given to them, and the penance or restitution they are asked to perform in consequence.

When the sacrament of reconciliation is mentioned, many Protestants are likely to give the speaker a blank look of incomprehension. The more informed might respond that these are Catholic things, and that Protestants – even Anglicans – don't regard reconciliation as a sacrament. There is a sense in which this is true. Article XXV of the XXXIX Articles shared the mainstream Reformation view that neither reconciliation, confirmation, anointing of the sick, marriage nor ordination are sacraments in the strict sense. Strictly speaking that honour belongs to baptism and eucharist alone, because only they are effective signs of grace and were clearly 'instituted' or commanded by Jesus himself. For each of the other five 'commonly called sacraments', one or both of these criteria is suspect.

In the case of reconciliation, it seems fairly difficult to dispute (assuming the substantial faithfulness of the gospel testimony) that Jesus entrusted some ministry of forgiveness to at least some among his followers: 'He breathed on them and said, "Receive the Holy Spirit. If you forgive the sins of any, they are forgiven; if you retain the sins of any, they are retained."' (See also Matthew 16.19; 18.15–18.) Importantly, these passages do not clearly demonstrate that ministry of forgiveness to be restricted only to the apostles, and by extension to the ministry which stands in succession from them. As will become apparent, debates about the sacramental status of reconciliation have been poisonously intertwined with debates about the nature of the ordained ministry: some have dismissed reconciliation in order to counter what were perceived to be noxious conceptions of ordination. One concern of this chapter will be to articulate the relationship between the two sacraments (which does indeed exist) in a way which takes some of the heat out of this controversy. The starting point, however, is uncontroversial and assured: Jesus entrusted a ministry of forgiveness to his Church.

Two important points – which will be familiar from thinking about baptism and the eucharist – are at stake in describing that ministry as 'sacramental'. First, it clarifies that reconciliation is never a purely private transaction between an individual believer and God. Just as people do not become or grow as Christians without the involvement of others, so they do not sin or receive forgiveness without others. All sins, even the most apparently private, are sins against the body of Christ: if for no other reason than that through their sin, the believer's unique contribution to the joy of the body is choked. 'They would not, without us, be made perfect' (Hebrews 11.40): as in the doctrine of eucharistic sacrifice, it matters for the salvation of all whether or not each one of us is truly saved. Individual sin wounds the whole body; therefore the whole body must somehow be involved in its healing.

Second, to describe reconciliation as sacramental means that it truly effects what it signifies. As the Church speaks and acts reconciliation with God – as the Church in the penitent confesses sin, and as the Church in the confessor speaks words of pardon and healing – joy happens: the wound created in the body of Christ through the sin of a Christian is healed. Note that this determines rather little – perhaps nothing – as to the precise form reconciliation must take. A certain basic pattern does seem to be required: there must be repentance, confession, absolution and penance. Each element in that pattern, however, could take a radically different form in different contexts. The pentitents' bench in a seventeenth-century Scots Presbyterian Kirk, where sinners publicly waited sometimes for months for their readmission to communion looks radically different from the curtained confessional box of modern Roman Catholicism. Arguably, however, both are just different manifestations of the one sacrament of reconciliation (even if the Scots Presbyterians would have vehemently rejected such terminology). Reconciliation, like all the sacraments, has unquestionably undergone considerable transformations throughout its history.

To begin at the beginning: already in 1 John we can see the struggles of the Church to come to terms with the enduring, impossible presence of sin within the body of Christ. A distinction emerges which quickly becomes of central importance in this history. 'If you see your brother or sister committing what is not a mortal sin, you will ask, and God will give him life to such a one – to those whose sin is not mortal. There is sin that is mortal; I do not say that you should pray about that' (1 John 5.16). 'John' doesn't elaborate, but clearly in his mind there are sins which are simply fatal, from which there can be no return (not all Christians share the hope of joy embracing all things!). Other, less serious, sins could be forgiven in part through the prayers of one's fellow disciples. This distinction was articulated by the early Church as one between 'mortal' and 'venial' sins. Mortal sins were widely understood as the big three: adultery, idolatry and murder. These sins killed the souls of any who committed them. With all lesser (venial) sins, there remained hope for repentance and restoration.

Very quickly, however, there was a further concession to reality. Bitter experience taught that baptized Christians committed not only venial, but mortal sins. Some in the Church – and there was fierce dispute on the point – dared to hope nonetheless that God could not wish even these to perish. Perhaps, just once in a lifetime, through repentance, confession and costly, long, public discipline even such lost souls could be restored. In the meantime – 15 years for adultery, say, in fourth-century Caesarea – they were excluded from the eucharist. The sinner has cut themselves off from joy, devastating the Church in the process. A long time is needed for wounds to heal, for some sort of restitution to be made and the life changed. At the end, the bishop would bring the sinner back and there would be great joy: but none should doubt that this was a once-only affair, a 'plank after shipwreck'.[42]

Alongside this, however, another tradition was growing up which was popularized by Irish monks (themselves influenced by eastern monasticism) in missions to continental Europe throughout the seventh century. They were concerned not just with rescuing Christians from the disaster of mortal sin but with encouraging growth in holiness,

42 The phrase is Tertullian's, cited in the *Catechism of the Catholic Church*, para. 1447, p. 325.

and saw real potential for this in the practice of confession and penance. Lesser sins, they thought, could be faced and extirpated through the regular practice of confessing and private penance. This did not involve excommunication – rather, it was intended to be part and parcel of normal Christian life, which should not rest content with anything less than perfection. Whatever its pastoral merits, this system of wholly private encounters between penitent and priest was far removed from the earlier discipline of public penitence. One scholar has noted that there is no evidence for anything like such a private system in the first five centuries of the Church: 'the first reliable evidence for private penance as a sacrament is found in Canon 2 of the third Council of Toledo (589) which castigates it as an "execrable presumption"'.[43] However, this was the practice that increasingly displaced the public system of penitence, and which was made obligatory for all western Christian adults once a year by the Lateran Council of 1215.

For some while longer, however, there was no precise, official clarity about exactly how this sacrament worked. It was fairly obvious that there were certain key elements involved in it: repentance, confession, absolution, restitution. However, the precise place and importance of each within the sacrament was unclear. In the East, it was quite common for restitution to be omitted altogether, as this element was regarded as perhaps suggesting too easily a 'box-ticking' exercise through which forgiveness was somehow mechanistically purchased. In the West, debate continued on how sincere someone's repentance needed to be (how could a confessor know? Indeed, how could the

---

43 J. N. D. Kelly, 1977, *Early Christian Doctrines*, 5th edn, London: A & C Black, p. 439.

penitent really know?), and whether the absolution pronounced by the priest was in any sense conditional.

The most influential view was put by Dun Scotus, who regarded the priest's words of absolution ('*ego te absolvo*' – 'I absolve you' being finally settled upon as the essential words or 'form' in this sacrament) as effective *ex opera operato*. This means that simply by virtue of these words being said by the authorized priest, the sins of the penitent were wiped away. Scotus' view held increasing sway in late medieval piety (despite diverging from no less an authority than Aquinas, who emphasized the absolute necessity of repentance). This is not necessarily evidence of moral laziness on the part of our predecessors: it could equally speak of the desperate desire for certainty of forgiveness, which could not be made to rest on anything so uncertain as the quality of one's inner dispositions. However, over time the Scotist view gave rise to the criticism that people could trot to confession daily to be forgiven, without the faintest intention of amending their lives – still a complaint often levelled today against the Roman Catholic practice of reconciliation.

The tension between Scotus and Thomas' position is of course not insuperable: the Church had already met and overcome a similar problem in baptismal theology. Centuries before, Augustine's case for not 're-baptizing' schismatics had been accepted: Donatist baptisms were real, but only came into full effect when the person joined the Catholic Church. One could argue that equally, in priestly absolution, sins are forgiven *ex opere operato*, but that repentance is needed for this forgiveness to be fully received. Indeed, this doctrine seems required by the gospel conviction that with God forgiveness always comes first – his 'attitude' towards us is always joyful grace, yearning to dissolve whatever barrier we put up. Divine absolution is never withheld, but always surges towards us. Through the words of the priest, it makes its powerful, all-but-irrestible appeal to us, to elicit and deepen our repentance. The sign is effective, forgiveness happens – but it avails us nothing unless we want it. And this, of course, means not only the desire not to be punished, but the desire for our sin to be washed away, for the ugly barriers raised against God and our neighbours to be dissolved. *That* will not happen without amendment of life and restitution. This indeed is what many in the late medieval Church taught, and what – too late – the Council of Trent made unmistakeably clear.

Too late, because the Reformation onslaught had already begun. Protestants found much to object to in the late medieval theory and practice of reconciliation – not least the fact that it was late and medieval, being found nowhere in Scripture or in the Fathers. However, they also considered it noxious. Just as in the case of the doctrine of eucharistic sacrifice, Protestants believed that Roman theology and practice appeared to undermine the basic fact of salvation: that Christ's death on the cross had availed once and for all for the forgiveness of all sins. No other human work was required: no sacrifice, no confession to a priest, no penance, but simply faith. Late medieval theology had spoken of the penitent making satisfaction for their sins through the penances imposed by the priest: this to the Reformers flew in the face of the gospel of justification by grace through faith alone.

To Protestant eyes, this deadly error was swiftly followed by another theological catastrophe. The Reformers believed that the Roman theology and practice of confession and penance was another instance of the ordained priesthood being made into a kind of intermediary between believers and God, endowed with quasi-magical powers. This encroached upon the dignity of the sole mediator, Jesus Christ, and seemed to reduce the laity to a dependent and inferior status in the body of Christ. This was objectionable at the best of times, and abhorrent when the clergy failed to manifest the kind of holiness and wisdom their exalted status suggested.

From the theological errors, moral and spiritual consequences flowed. To Protestants, confession and penance as practised in the late medieval Church appeared to allow the religiously insincere the comfort of thinking that they could pop into confession at any time, be absolved and carry on sinning. Protestants of course believed that grace was given freely, without any work of ours, but they believed equally strongly that grace brought with it a real transformation of life. Like Paul, they found the idea that those touched by grace could go on sinning abhorrent. The confessional seemed to invite that abuse. As for the religiously sincere, however, Catholic practice made them think they had to earn God's forgiveness through the dutiful performance of penance. The dutiful Augustinian monk, Martin Luther, knew that way lay failure and misery: his consequent vehement rejection of penance was one of the immediate causes of the Reformation.

Nevertheless, the various Protestant traditions still understood the value of one Christian telling another of their sins and receiving from that person assurance of Christ's forgiveness. There was still something that bore some resemblance to confession and reconciliation in their corporate lives. It was however the differences from the old practices which were most obvious. No Protestant taught that private confession was obligatory, or that the minister in such situations did more than declare what Christ had already done for sinners on the cross. Nothing happened in confession which could not happen in private prayer, and indeed in most circumstances it was considered better if it *did* happen in private prayer. The believer should not need anyone else to broker the relationship with God. Accordingly, Lutheran and Calvinist traditions firmly avoided the '*ego te absolvo*' formula in such pastoral encounters, and were largely indifferent to whether the confessor was an ordained minister or not.

The Church of England was part of this Reformed consensus, although as in other respects less thoroughgoingly so than many Puritans and continental reformers would have liked. The BCP's First Exhortation to Holy Communion encourages any who by private prayer are unable to quiet their consciences to go to a 'discreet and learned Minister of God's Word, and open his grief; that by the ministry of God's holy Word he may receive the benefit of absolution, together with ghostly counsel and advice'. The Order for the Visitation of the Sick goes further, retaining a rite of private confession and absolution including the 'I absolve thee' form. Much later, some determined Anglo-Catholics would implausibly claim that by doing so it effectively made room for the late medieval understanding of reconciliation. Yet this is to ignore the obvious fact that the English Reformers were largely as hostile as their continental counterparts to the Roman theology of priesthood, and the clear denial in the XXXIX Articles that confession is a sacrament. Moreover use of this rite remained strictly optional. Even in the wake of the nineteenth-century Catholic revival in Anglicanism which vigorously promoted confession, the Anglican tradition as a whole never really embraced it. It is not 'the Anglican position' on confession but only the Anglo-Catholic one which could be accurately described with the oft-cited maxim: 'All may, some should, none must.'

If Protestantism gave one withering critique of confession and absolution, the place of this sacrament in contemporary Christian life has been at least equally devastated by another principal factor: secularization. This is the 300-year process by which, gradually but inexorably, the whole of European culture has ceased to imagine itself as involved with God. One especially potent element in that process was the European Enlightenment's determination to reimagine humanity in fundamentally optimistic terms. For too long, it was claimed, religion had held back progress by obsessing about guilt, keeping people in fear of hell and in tutelage to their clergy. Humanity needed to throw off these humiliating chains, and to realize its innate goodness and boundless promise. Things could only get better.

In this brave new dawn, few doctrines were exposed to such scorching criticism as the old Augustinian doctrine of original sin with its dark pessimism regarding human moral possibilities since the Fall. Over time, that criticism successfully reshaped the European imagination, so that the sense of crushing personal guilt expressed, for example, in Cranmer's *Book of Common Prayer* is simply no longer instinctively felt by our culture as a whole. When individuals *do* feel it, the culture (even the Church) is as likely to judge this pathological as to accept it as a realistic picture of the self. Confession and absolution of sin is seldom seen as the remedy: rather, the individual is encouraged to be easier on themselves, to understand the limits imposed on their responsibility by genetics, early nurture, social conditioning and economic circumstance. If the spirit remains troubled, then psychotherapists and drugs are increasingly seen as more fitted to the task than priests and their rituals. The drama of reconciliation is not seen as being between the soul and God, but as within the divided psyche. The consulting room, almost everywhere, replaced the confessional.

The practice of confession presented an easy target for enlightened scorn in the West. Increasingly understood as a Roman Catholic practice only (for only they insisted upon it), the role of the priest in this sacrament attracted almost the same vehemence from secularists as from Protestants. How dare one man presume to forgive the sins of another? It seemed to imply that the priest was somehow spiritually superior – an attitude which celibacy and endemic clerical arrogance did little to dispel. An increasingly educated and self-confident laity would have little truck with this, and fell away from regular confession. Furthermore, these celibate confessors were (sometimes fairly, sometimes not so) imagined to be pruriently preoccupied with sexual 'sins' – increasingly even committed Catholics were unsure what these might be, doubtful of the clergy's competence to pronounce about them, and finally appalled to discover the existence of widespread sexual abuse by priests. The recent scandals and perceived 'cover-up' have probably dealt a death blow to whatever (very) residual confidence in confession the mass of Western European Catholics retained after centuries of Protestant and secular scorn.

Which is of course ironic, because what these scandals reveal is the horrible mystery of evil in the human heart and the Church which confession and absolution were meant to address. Enlightened optimism may have scorned the doctrine of original sin but, as G. K. Chesterton said, of all Christian doctrines it is the one most clearly supported by the facts.[44] The faith that left to their own devices humans and their societies will develop in benign, peaceful, progressive ways must be by now among the most evidently bankrupt creeds ever adopted. It was not religion which planned the Holocaust, ran the Gulag and dropped the bomb. The Enlightenment had valid criticisms of the Church, and made many great achievements (there were vaccines as well as bombs), but it ended teaching a lesson it did not believe: that there is a dark strain of misery and violence running stubbornly and inextricably deep within us all, personally and corporately. And this, Christians call sin.

Given this, there is a lot to be said for a creative retrieval of what the Church has historically tried to do in the sacrament of reconciliation. And, indeed, within the overall story of decline which we have traced, there are significant shoots of growth to be noted. The great Lutheran theologian Dietrich Bonhoeffer strongly advocated the practice of confession describing it as 'a renewal of the joy of baptism'.[45] For large numbers of Anglicans sacramental confession or something very like it happens in informal spiritual direction and pastoral care. Many evangelical churches encourage their members to discuss their failings fully and freely with a small group of Christian friends, for mutual support and assurance of God's mercy. Albeit carefully stripped of any sense of absolute obligation or priestly mediation of forgiveness, all these trends point to a hunger among Protestants for something of what was meant to happen in the sacrament of reconciliation.

44 G. K. Chesterton, 1999, *Orthodoxy*, London: Hodder and Stoughton, p. 10.

45 Dietrich Bonhoeffer, 1954, *Life Together*, London: SCM Press, p. 90.

Meanwhile in the Roman Catholic tradition, there has recently been experimentation with corporate services of reconciliation, in which people may confess privately to the priest as the whole church celebrates an act of repentance and worship. Some conservative Catholics have reacted cautiously to the great popularity of such services, fearing that it may represent the indulgence of a preference for 'confession-lite' which dispenses with the obligation to confess one's sins fully and frankly to the priest. There is probably an element of truth in that, but a 'glass half-full' approach might rather choose to celebrate the fact that these services are clearly meeting a felt need among many Catholics to express repentance and receive absolution. We might even rejoice that these services give expression to two fundamental realities perhaps somewhat eclipsed by the private confessions of individuals to a priest. First, there is the thoroughly Pauline emphasis on the ecclesial dimension of sin and forgiveness: the ancient recognition that my sin is not just my problem but blights the whole Church, and that the whole Church must pray for me to be forgiven and rejoice when I am. Second, such services can speak powerfully to the sense that some of the things of which there is most need to repent today do not pertain exclusively, or even primarily, to individual responsibility. The unjust distribution of resources across the world (for instance) is not the fault of any one individual. It is precisely as a member of the community that the individual is responsible, and it is the community of individuals which needs to repent, be forgiven and make restitution. So if there is going to be a revival of this sacrament in the life of the Western Church, services like these may well be the place to look.

There are then some positive signs for the sacrament of reconciliation even today. However, it has to be admitted that for most Christians today all this is still more than faintly exotic, alien even. For all the reasons we have traced, not forgetting the simple fact that it is deeply uncomfortable, sacramental reconciliation is not seen by most believers now as an integral and unremarkable part of discipleship. This is understandable, but a great shame.

It is a shame because when it is done properly – in repentance, with firm intention to change one's life – confession and absolution are one of the great ways in which the joy of Jesus breaks into our lives. Of course, from the Anglican and Protestant perspective, no one *has* to choose this way. It is indeed possible to know the forgiveness of God solely through the private prayer of penitence, exposing oneself before God without the need for any human mediation. On the other hand, however, there are good reasons for suggesting that human mediation – and not only that, but the ministry of an ordained priest – can be very helpful indeed. We may not be obliged to practise confession, nor are we generally obliged to receive great gifts, but usually we reach for them with joy!

Regular confession of our sins to another person is a great gift for several reasons. First, because in private prayer we sometimes find it difficult to distinguish between talking to God and talking to ourselves. It is rather easy for the prayer of penitence to turn simply into a litany of how terrible we are, and not to hear the word of forgiveness spoken from beyond. The other person can help to make God real, simply by not being us. Second, because the other great temptation in private prayer is to not quite name the true darkness of our sin, to hide behind generalized expressions of regret. A wise confessor can gently prod and draw out the full meaning of what we fear to say. Or indeed, sometimes, they can gently suggest that perhaps our secrets are not that devastatingly sinful after all.

A related point is that the experience of confessing to another Christian is indeed truly humiliating, in the good and proper sense that it makes us humble. Another person, like me, knows the worst. It is somehow often easier to tell God the worst, because (at least in the most obvious – but perhaps ultimately misleading – sense) God isn't sitting there looking back. But this person is, and she knows my true nature. There can be no pretence now that I am other than what I am: a sinner, fallen far short of the glory of God. However, if she is a good confessor then her whole being and demeanour will make real for me the words of absolution which she speaks. I *know* I am forgiven, because this other person, knowing the worst, reaches out with compassion to tell me that, even so, I am loved by God and by them.

And this, to reiterate, is the strongest reason for describing reconciliation as a sacrament. In all this, joy has been taking flesh. There is no bread, or wine, or water here but there are human words and gestures: the sign of the cross, the embrace. Human communication, so often the raw material for deceit, is in this moment the vehicle of joy. The barriers of secrecy and pride which I have built around myself through my sin are dissolved by my words of confession, and joy rushes in to rebuild communion through the words of absolution. The sign is effective: joy happens. Perhaps the deepest shame in the widespread decline of confession is that so many Christians simply don't get to feel this.

The final important benefit of confessing to another person rather than in the secrecy of private prayer goes back to the insight of those early Irish missionaries that reconciliation was integral to a Christian's growth in holiness. For many, 'ghostly counsel' (as Cranmer famously described the advice the minister might give the penitent) has proved almost as valuable as the words of absolution. The confessor can be far more insightful and wise about our predicament than we ourselves, and – if they're gifted in this ministry – suggest ways of tackling the patterns of sinfulness exposed in the confession. This is where the element of penance comes in, as something so much more creative and healing than the 'price list' approach so easily parodied ('Feelings of envy? Five Hail Marys!'). The wise confessor suggests something that will help make the desire for change real, turn 'wish' into flesh (something of a theme in sacramental theology, and the best response to the Protestant fear that penance is seen as 'earning' God's favour).

So much for the benefits of confession to another disciple. What of the more controversial claim, that it is of especial benefit to confess to an ordained priest? Traditional Roman Catholic thought holds that this is essential, because the priest alone (by virtue of his ordination to the apostolic ministry) stands *in persona Christi.* Only his actions – whether in offering the eucharist, or absolving sins – are therefore certain to be the actions of Jesus. We offered some criticism of this view in our chapter on the eucharist, and will explore it further when dealing with ordination – but suffice it to say we do not adopt it here.

There is, however, another rationale that can be offered. Leave on one side, for the moment, what we would hope is true: that priests will simply be the kind of people who are good at this ministry – wise, compassionate, steeped in prayer. Hopefully they are, but the significance of their ordination for reconciliation goes beyond this. Consider instead what the inward and spiritual reality happening in reconciliation is: Jesus joyously reclaiming into his life one who had begun to sever himself from it through sin. The whole Church has suffered through that drifting away, because the Church is a body – a deep sharing of lives made gifts one to another, making each other alive with the joy of Jesus. When a sinner withdraws, the body is wounded. When they are reconciled, the whole body rejoices.

If this is the inward and spiritual reality, how best to give it outward and visible expression? More of this in a later chapter, but we suggest that making the ordained priest the normal minister of reconciliation is a most obvious way for two reasons. First, that person represents through their ordination not only the local congregation, but that congregation's belonging within the great communion of saints across time and space. He or she is one of the ways in which the spiritual reality of that great communion is made public and visible – once again, the sacramental principle is at work. It is also at work in reconciliation, when the involvement of the ordained minister symbolizes and effects the involvement of the whole body in the loss and recovery of one of its members.

Second, with the symbolic role of the ordained in the life of the body come particular responsibilities and functions. Their overall task is to effect what they signify: the knitting of the local and particular congregation and every person within it into the great communion. Through liturgical leadership, preaching, teaching, pastoral care and prayer the priest is responsible for helping the body to be fully itself. What belongs more naturally with this than to be the one who enacts for the sinner his reconciliation with Jesus and his people?

None of this implies, of course, that the priest has any sort of special powers held apart from the rest of the Church. Nor, emphatically, are they better than anyone else (a point beautifully and made simply by the words of dismissal in many rites of reconciliation: 'Your sins are put away. Go in peace, and pray for me a sinner also'). There is no suggestion that reconciliation without an ordained priest is somehow not 'real', or that if one had to choose between confessing to a wise, gentle, prayerful layperson or a boorish priest one should choose the priest! The claim is simply that all other things being equal, what is really happening is given best expression through an ordained priest doing it. And that matters because it is when things are given best expression that we stand the best chance of absorbing what they mean. The joy of reconciliation is so great that we do ourselves a disservice by selling it short.

FOR DISCUSSION

- '. . . we acknowledge and bewail our manifold sins and wickedness, which we from time to time most grievously have committed, by thought, by word and by deed, against thy divine majesty, provoking most justly thy wrath and indignation against us . . . the remembrance of them is grievous unto us, the burden of them is intolerable' (BCP Holy Communion). Is this an exaggeration?
- How does your church deal with serious sin?
- What is the difference between a priest and a psychotherapist?
- Is confession always good for the soul?
- Are there unforgiveable sins, and what might they be?

FOR REFLECTION

No Christian is an evildoer. If he were, his membership would be mere sham.
Athenagoras[46]

46 Athenagoras, *A Plea for the Christians* 2,3, cited in Martin Dudley and Geoffrey Rowell, 1990, *Confession and Absolution*, London: SPCK, p. 40.

Sooner or later, we must all drive into the extermination camp and confront without illusion the most unbearable truth about what it is to be human, the truth that benevolence and rationality are not at the heart of people's actions. There is a horror of great darkness in our dealings with each other.
Rowan Williams[47]

After this reconciliation with God, pious men, who approach this sacrament, holily and devoutly, sometimes experience the greatest peace and tranquillity of conscience, accompanied with the highest spiritual delight. For there is no crime, however grievous, however revolting, which the sacrament of penance does not remit, not once only, but often and repeatedly.
Council of Trent[48]

Here shall the sick person be moved to make a special confession of his sins, if he feels his conscience to be troubled with any weighty matter. After which, the Priest shall absolve him (if he humbly and heartily desire it), after this sort: 'Our Lord Jesus Christ who hath left power to his Church, to absolve all sinners who truly repent and believe in him, of his great mercy forgive thee thine offences: And by his authority committed to me, I absolve thee from all thy sins. In the Name of the Father, and of the Son, and of the Holy Ghost. Amen.
Book of Common Prayer, *Visitation of the Sick*

47 Rowan Williams, 1994, *Open to Judgement: Sermons and Addresses*, London: Darton, Longman and Todd, p. 89.

48 Council of Trent, *Decree on Sacrament of Penance*, Ch. 18.

We (the Church of England) stand chiefly upon the true, inward conversion of the heart; (the Roman Catholic Church) more upon works of external show. We teach, above all things, that repentance which is one and the same from the beginning to the world's end; they a sacramental penance of their own devising and shaping. We labour to instruct men in such sort, that every soul which is wounded with sin may learn the way how to cure itself; they, clean contrary, would make all sores seem uncurable, unless the priest have a hand in them.
Richard Hooker[49]

When (Jesus Christ's) ear is deaf, and his heart is cold – when his hand is feeble, and his power to heal is exhausted – when the treasure house of his sympathy is empty, and his love and good will have become cold – then, and not till then, it will be time to turn to earthly priests and earthly confessionals. Thank God, that time is not yet come!
J. C. Ryle[50]

. . . we must ask ourselves whether we have not often been deceiving ourselves with our confession of sin to God, whether we have not rather been confessing our sins to ourselves and perhaps granting ourselves absolution. And is not the reason perhaps for our countless relapses and the feebleness of our Christian obedience to be found precisely in the fact that we are living on self-forgiveness, and not real forgiveness? Self-forgiveness

---

49 Richard Hooker, *Laws of Ecclesiastical Polity*, Book VI: 6,2.

50 Cited in John Stott, 1964, *Confess Your Sins: The Way of Reconciliation*, London: Hodder and Stoughton, p. 68.

can never lead to a breach with sin; this can only be accomplished by the judging and pardoning Word of God itself . . . a man who confesses his sin in the presence of a brother knows he is no longer alone with himself; he experiences the presence of God in the reality of the other person.
Dietrich Bonhoeffer[51]

51 Dietrich Bonhoeffer, 1954, *Life Together*, London: SCM Press, pp. 90–1.

5

Joy heals (II): Anointing the sick

Perhaps we fret too much about the decline of the sacrament of reconciliation. Not only does it yet show some signs of vitality, as traced in the last chapter, but its twin sacrament has experienced a great revival in the course of the twentieth century and into our own. From great Catholic shrines such as Lourdes, through the rise of Charismatic Renewal (that movement which places so much emphasis upon the lively presence of the Holy Spirit in worship, made known in deeds of power) across all denominations, through to quiet services of healing in utterly 'middle-of-the-road' traditional parish churches: the ministry of healing is everywhere you look. And while not all – perhaps relatively few – of those involved in this ministry would necessarily express themselves in such terms, what they are doing frequently looks a great deal like one of the traditional seven sacraments of the Church: the anointing of the sick.

Strictly speaking, at least if we follow the lead of the Roman Catholic Church, this sacrament must involve the anointing of the sick person with oil, considered as part of the essential outward reality of the inner and spiritual reality. We will see that the use of oil is indeed richly appropriate in the ministry of healing. However, our focus will be on healing more generally, considered as a sacrament with or without the use of oil. For the primary 'outward and visible sign' of the joy communicated through this ministry is surely what happens in the suffering of the one to whom healing is offered. As in reconciliation, the sacramental 'matter' here is not (exclusively or necessarily) a physical substance, but a transformed human situation.

Reconciliation and healing of course belonged together in the ministry of Jesus: 'When Jesus saw their faith, he said to the paralytic, "Son, your sins are forgiven"' (Mark 2.5). Apparently, in this case, Jesus diagnosed the root cause of the man's paralysis as sin. The scribes object not to the diagnosis, but to Jesus' presuming to declare the sin removed. Jesus then proves his point by saying to the sick man, 'rise, take your pallet, and go home', which he does. In other cases of healing, there is no reference to sin causing the condition (e.g. Luke 8.43–48). However, there is little doubt that in Jesus' mind and those of his contemporaries, sin and sickness were to say the least closely allied powers, twin manifestations of the great failure of Israel and of the world to be as God intended. The dawning of the Kingdom must mean the end of both. Jesus' healings then were good news not just in themselves, but because they represented the Kingdom beginning to happen, joy erupting in the midst of failure. Can Jesus really be the Messiah? 'Go and tell John what you hear and see: the blind receive their sight, the lame walk, the lepers are cleansed, the deaf hear, the dead are raised, and the poor have good news brought to them' (Matthew 11.4–5).

The Church was meant to be the people in and through whom joy went on happening, in and through whom Jesus went on rejoicing the world back to God. Naturally, then, it should bring healing. This is precisely what we find Jesus sending his apostles to do: 'So they went out and proclaimed that all should repent. They cast out many demons, and anointed with oil many that were sick and cured them' (Mark 6.12–13). We read of healings in the Acts of the Apostles (9.32–35; 14.8–10). Paul includes healing among the gifts of the Spirit in 1 Corinthians 12.9, and 'James' assures us: 'Are any among you sick? They should call for the elders of the church and have them pray over them, anointing them with oil in the name of the Lord. The prayer of faith will save the sick, and the Lord will raise them up; and anyone who has committed sins will be forgiven' (James 5.14–15).

From the last chapter we remember the criteria by which something 'counts' as a sacrament: it must be entrusted to the Church by Jesus and it must be an effective sign, actually bringing what it signifies into existence. It would seem difficult to deny then that healing is a sacrament of the Church – and yet, this is precisely what happened at the Reformation. Calvin declared that healing had ceased in the time of the apostles, and the English Book of Common Prayer omitted any rite of healing from its office for the Visitation of the Sick (which, remember, included provision for confession and absolution). How did this happen to a practice with such apparently impeccable scriptural warrant?

Perhaps the most obvious explanation is that healing simply didn't seem to work – it *wasn't* an effective sign, in that most of those who received it continued to sicken and then to die. Nor had it taken until the sixteenth century for this fact to dawn upon people. Calvin was right to say that beyond the apostolic era there is not much evidence of a widespread ministry of healing in the Church. What happened instead was that the ritual of anointing with prayer and laying on of hands had been put to a rather different purpose: that of preparing Christians in the face of imminent death. Because of this the sacrament came to be known by an alternative title, 'extreme unction'. In the 1960s, the Second Vatican Council reminded the church of the sacrament's original, wider scope: however, even today the *Catechism of the Catholic Church* teaches that this sacrament is most appropriately given when death begins to threaten through serious illness.[52] This distinguishes the sacramental anointing of the sick from many other manifestations of the Church's healing ministry. The sacrament's primary intention is not to cure the sick, but enable believers to sicken and die gracefully – more of this anon.

The Reformers could reject extreme unction as a sacrament because it was difficult to show that Jesus had commanded it. Furthermore, it seemed unnecessary. What grace was given to the Christian here that had not already been given in baptism and eucharist, what consolation not given by good pastoral care? Reformers also worried that the practice bred superstition and 'priestcraft': people might believe that somehow without the ministry of a priest and his ritual in the last moments, their salvation was somehow imperilled. Uncommanded, unnecessary and misleading: in the Reformers' minds extreme unction and anointing of the sick were obvious candidates for pruning.

Now, however, this judgement seems ripe for reconsideration. The last century has seen an explosion of interest in the healing ministry of the Church, and within this of the place of anointing and laying on of hands. Certainly in the Protestant world, this might be viewed as an especially striking example of 'the return of the repressed': four long centuries of anti-sacramentalism and rationalist modes of

52 *Catechism of the Catholic Church*, para. 1514, p. 339.

thought distrustful of religious experience suddenly giving way to the Charismatic Renewal of the twentieth century. Other factors might include an increasing sense among many as the twentieth century progressed that medical science did not hold all the answers to the problems of the body. The application of scientific method and technology to human healing had clearly achieved amazing things, but the claim that the body could be comprehensively mastered by such methods remained implausible. In many quarters (not just religious) there was a renewed interest in health as a condition of the whole person, seen not just as a machine but a complex psychosomatic unity. Increasing awareness and understanding of mental illness was only one part of this newly broadened vision.

Intriguingly, we might also claim the very decline in the sacrament of reconciliation as a factor in the increase of the healing ministry. The Letter of James and the stories of Jesus' healings make clear how, from the very beginning, the Christian instinct has been to put sin and sickness together. This is not necessarily in the crude sense that each sickness is a tailor-made 'punishment' for particular sin. Rather it is the recognition, on the one hand, that these evils belong together as the opposite of joy, and that in some cases there does seem to be if not straightforward causality at work then a complex, subtle mutual reinforcing of sin and sickness. Many doctors, for example, recognize that Jesus' question to one crippled man, 'Do you want to be made well?' (John 5.6), is not stupid cruelty, but often a very pertinent spur to healing.

It might well be, then, that as one sacrament seemed to dry up as a means by which joy might redeem human misery, it was time for the other to come back into prominence. What's more, perhaps the sacrament of healing is in some ways better suited to our felt predicament than that of reconciliation, at least as the latter has traditionally been practised. Leaving on one side the fact that we will always like to avoid full and frank confession, it is also true that for many what needs relief is not so much a particular, clearly identified sin (these can often seem rather trival and pathetic) as a more generalized sense of tawdriness and failure. It is not that this *doesn't* require confession and absolution, rather that these need to be part of a more general 'raising up of ruins' which seems better expressed in the rite of healing. It is also arguable that in this way the sacrament of reconciliation may come into clearer focus as the means by which only especially grievous sins are normally addressed.

Given this revival of the healing ministry in the Church, what are we to make of the obvious objection that most of the time it doesn't seem to work? The same problem applies of course to baptism, which claims to make us new yet apparently fails to do so. In the case of baptism, we argued that this required an eschatological reference – in other words, that baptism should be considered as effective in that it really plants within us a dynamism and energy which cannot but come to fruition in the Kingdom. Sin may linger, but its reign is over and it will be driven out. Healing may be effective in just the same way. Sickness may remain, and death certainly still awaits. That was true even for those whom Jesus brought back from the dead. That, however, does not mean that his signs were undone or defeated. They stood as promises of the greater healing to come beyond history, the Kingdom of God in which all sin and death would be destroyed.

So the efficacy of anointing is not to be judged by the absence of obvious, immediate healing in those to whom it is given. Joy, planted in us, will come to its fullness only in the end of all things. On the other hand – and again like baptism – it would be disturbing if there was *no* power communicated now through the action, no discernible impact in the lives of those who receive the sacrament. Joy *happens* through what Jesus does in his Church. The baptized are launched into a life of growing holiness. So, too, anointing will bear fruit. However, remembering the deep kinship of this sacrament with that of reconciliation, it would be wise to see the healing conferred through it as usually a process rather than an event: grace is not likely to 'zap' a problem like keyhole laser surgery, but will rather gradually renew the afflicted nature. Equally, like reconciliation, it simply will not take hold without the will of the patient to be well or the will of the Church to support the healing process. Yet when this sacrament is used responsibly, especially in cases of mental distress and psychosomatic illnesses, we have every reason to hope for measurable and significant improvement.

Some extraordinary times, such improvement might come in the most obvious and immediate sense. Scientific rationalism should not cow us into refusing to recognize that sometimes pain does retreat, and tumours do disappear. To say so is not to rush headlong into credulous acceptance of every claimed healing, nor to deny that ordinarily such healing is going to come through the skill and care of medical professionals. Scepticism towards claims of the miraculous, and trust in doctors, are both deeply sane and Christian instincts. However, there is simply too much both in the Scriptures and contemporary Christian experience to rule out a priori the possibility that joy does extraordinary things. To deny the category of miracle altogether seems impossible for someone who takes the gospel stories of Jesus seriously.

On the other hand, one day even those so healed will still sicken and die. Thus it was a very sound theological instinct which drove the Church over the centuries to locate the primary use of the sacrament of healing near the end of the Christian's life, as death loomed. This made clear that ultimately what this sacrament means, and what Christians hope for, is not that we will not be sick or that we will not die. Sickness and death are not going to be abolished this side of the Kingdom, any more than bread and wine are abolished in the eucharist. Rather, in both cases what happens is that the ordinary human significance of things is transfigured, made to convey new meanings. In the eucharist, bread and wine speak of a joy and sharing far beyond their normal use as means of survival and acquisition. In this sacrament, suffering and mortality, which can so easily plunge the person into isolation, fear, anger and resentment, are to be changed. Healing in the face of death looks like acceptance, patience, gentleness. It looks like communion, as the dying are held physically and spiritually by the whole Church, and as in their graceful dying they teach those who come after how to die in Christ.

We touch here, incidentally, on why anointing with oil is such a deeply appropriate part of this sacrament. Oil had long served in the ancient world as a highly effective way of protecting a wound from infection, so there was a certain obviousness in the Church's symbolic use of it in healing. However, oil was also used to anoint those summoned to special tasks such as kingship or priesthood, and significantly for the preparation of bodies before burial. The latter, of course, marked the action Jesus praised the anonymous woman for at Bethany (Mark 14.8). In each case, the common idea seems to be that of preparing the anointed one to face an awesome task. For the Christian, the symbolism is reinforced by the custom of anointing in Christian initiation (whether as part of the baptismal ritual, or in the separate act of confirmation). Anointing with oil at initiation spoke of being empowered by the Spirit to share in the life of Jesus, commissioned to pour out his joy to the world. In being anointed as death looms, our fundamental baptismal anointing is refreshed and reoriented towards the climactic act of the Christian's sharing in Jesus, entering fully in his death. Not for nothing does traditional Catholic piety sometimes speak of death as 'the completion of baptism'.

Why is this the climax? Because in death, all that has been spoken of in the sacramental life comes to its fulfilment. In the last chapter, we spoke of Jesus' death as a sacrifice: as the great consummation of his pouring out of himself in joy so that others might rejoice. Death is when there is nothing left of him but joy, which then begins to undo the power of death from within. What had been the ruin of human community, severing each from all others eternally, has been changed by his death into communion beyond our wildest imaginings – into what we falteringly call 'resurrection' and 'eternal life'. Death is no longer the great enemy, but what St Francis called 'Sister Death': the graceful moment when finally all that holds us back from utter immersion in the great joy which is God, the great act of self-sharing, is dissolved. My very existence, conceived of as my own and to some degree held apart from everyone else's, ends. This is the culmination of what baptism and the eucharist have tried to teach me, and to some extent have begun within me: that ultimately my deepest joy, the most truly personal joy, will come when every trace of ego and self-preservation has been emptied out. In a sense, I must die so that Christ can live through me. 'I' as ego must die so that the greater mystery of 'I', the self that God created me to be and not the self that sin asserted, can live. When a life trained by baptism and discipleship faces its end, physical death becomes simply the outward sign of an inward and spiritual grace. Death is God's last great gift: the translation of life into pure joy. If anointing with oil helps us embrace *that*, it truly deserves its place among the sacraments of the Church.

Exorcism

It would be wrong to leave the sacrament of anointing without dealing briefly with a significant action closely related to it and the subject (often for very bad reasons) of great fascination: exorcism. Technically, exorcism is not one of the seven sacraments – although that only shows the limitations of an overly rigid enumeration of sacraments, as it is very difficult to understand why exorcism shouldn't count. There can be no real question that the New Testament understands Jesus to have cast out evil spirits himself, and to have commissioned his disciples to do the same (Mark 6.7–13; 16.17 – significantly, just the same texts cited in the case of anointing). Nor can it be doubted that exorcism was believed to constitute an effective sign. There is no good reason why it should not be counted as a sacrament.

A perfectly valid reason for *not* counting it among the seven is to say that it is simply a dimension within either the sacrament of reconciliation or the sacrament of anointing. It would also of course be theologically sound to press beyond this and say that these sacraments are nothing of themselves, but simply signify and bring out the power given in baptism. And indeed we discover that the liturgy of baptism is just where exorcism still makes its appearance within the ordinary life of the Church today. Candidates are normally to be signed with the cross; they renounce Satan, and the priest prays that they shall be delivered from the powers of darkness. Most churches, therefore, exorcise on a regular basis without giving it a second thought!

However, an at least equally powerful reason for the neglect of exorcism in contemporary sacramental theology is not so valid. The famous twentieth-century theologian Rudolf Bultmann famously put it thus: 'It is impossible to use electric light and the wireless and to avail ourselves of modern medical and surgical discoveries, and at the same time to believe in the New Testament world of spirits and miracles.'[53] Most would not go all the way with Bultmann, but demons frequently seem a bridge too far even for those Christians who have not succumbed to Enlightenment sneering at all the supernatural aspects of the faith. Exorcism, accordingly, seems to many an embarrassment to the Church rather than a gift. However, it should also be noted that like healing more generally it has enjoyed something of a revival among churches of the Charismatic Renewal, and in a more understated way in traditional churches such as the Church of England, where every diocese now has an authorized 'ministry of deliverance'. Not all of this is healthy, but at least some of it suggests another instance of the principle that there are things which the Church simply needs and which cannot vanish from its life for long.

The position here is parallel to that of healing miracles. A good deal of scepticism should be applied to claims of

53 Rudolf Bultmann, 1941, 'New Testament and Mythology', in Hans W. Bartsch, ed., 1961, *Kerygma and Myth: A Theological Debate by Rudolf Bultmann and Five Critics*, New York: Harper and Brothers, pp. 1–44, p. 5.

demonic activity – not least because churches have shown themselves to be deeply irresponsible, sometimes fatally so, in their handling of presumed 'possession'. Frequently, there will be perfectly satisfactory explanations for spiritual distress which need no recourse to the demonic, and on the basis of which sufferers can be effectively relieved. Scepticism towards demonology is an essential requirement of anyone involved in the Church's healing ministry. Certainly, exorcism should not be used before doctors and psychiatrists have been closely involved with a case.

Scepticism, however, is not the same thing as a closed mind. The Church may have frequently got things disastrously wrong in its judgements about the demonic, and belief in little horned creatures with burning eyes and pitchforks is clearly ridiculous. However, we should pause to consider whether our ancestors were truly credulous enough to take such imagery literally themselves. Was it not always intended to express rather what the New Testament tries to point towards with its own language of evil spirits, principalities and powers: namely the great energies of darkness and destruction which seem to surge into lives from somewhere beyond rational human choice? *That* perception seems too deeply embedded in the New Testament to be casually discarded in pursuit of a 'core message' more acceptable to the standards of contemporary scientific rationality.

We should also avoid the habit of making the demonic ridiculous by confining it to the more exotic and spectacular cases so beloved of sensationalist films and novels. If there is a great power of destruction and darkness, it is at least as likely to be found working its way through much more grimly mundane realities. Think of things like anorexia – that frightening, uncontrollable self-destruction which is beyond all reasoning, which drives people to death. Or of the despair which drives people into the various addictions which surround us – drink, drugs, work, gambling. Or of the urges which took people who were presumably once decent and turned them into compulsive paedophiles. Of course, rational scientific, medical, sociological and psychological analyses have taught us a great deal about all these afflictions, and of course we would be criminally foolish to discard their work. But we may reasonably question whether in the end they do any more than show us some of the workings of evil. These disciplines end up seeming to point to something rather like what Christians have traditionally meant by demonology: to something deeper and wilder than deliberate choice (although not utterly divorced from it either), to a power of miserable destruction which holds with a seemingly inexorable grip.

Against such powers of darkness, there *might* come a time when, alongside and in co-ordination with professional therapy and other treatment, exorcism becomes a sensible measure. Such a measure could of course only be taken with the most extreme caution and care, after slow discernment by people who know the case exceptionally well. Given that exorcism is a dimension of the sacraments of reconciliation and healing, like them it will almost certainly reveal its true force only as part of a process, and only as the person involved is consistently accompanied and supported on their journey towards healing and freedom. Joy does not normally 'zap' (though it can!). But when used with all due wisdom, only unreasonable rationalism could deny exorcism its place within the sacraments of the Church. Joy knows its enemy, and if necessary, it will drive him out.

FOR DISCUSSION

- Why does God seem to heal some, but not others?
- Are mental illnesses more likely to be helped by the Church's healing ministry than physical ones, and if so why?
- How does your church help people to die?
- What do you think a demon is?

FOR REFLECTION

. . . by the operation of the Holy Ghost, the Comforter, this oil may avail for the healing of all infirmities. To all who receive it, and put their trust in thy mercy, may this anointing be a heavenly medicine, a spiritual remedy, an inward and abiding unction, unto the strengthening and healing of soul and mind and body, and the renewal of the Holy Ghost in thy living temple.
The Sarum Pontifical, liturgy for the blessing of oils for the anointing of the sick[54]

Night is drawing nigh.
For all that has been – Thanks!
To all that shall be – Yes!
Dag Hammarskjold[55]

---

54 Cited in C. W. Gusmer, 1974, *The Ministry of Healing in the Church of England: An Ecumenical-Liturgical Study*, London: Mayhew-McCrimon, pp. 103–4.

55 Dag Hammarskjöld, 1964, *Markings*, London: Faber and Faber, p. 14.

How wonderful it is, is it not, that literally only Christianity has taught us the true peace and function of suffering. The Stoics tried the hopeless little game of denting its objective reality . . . and the Pessimists attempted to revel in it . . . but Christ came, and he did not really explain it; he did far more, he met it, willed it, transformed it, and he taught us how to do all this, or rather he himself does it within us, if we do not hinder the all healing hands . . .
Friedrich von Hugel[56]

[Approaching death] we are surrounded by the invisible and silent company of all who have found eternal life in this life and death of ours, and who have allowed themselves to be wholly absorbed into this mystery which softly and silently detaches us from ourselves (the mystery we usually call God).
Karl Rahner[57]

56 Cited in Martin Dudley and Geoffrey Rowell, eds, 1993, *The Oil of Gladness: Anointing in the Christian Tradition*, London: SPCK, p. 154.

57 Karl Rahner, 1977, *Meditations on the Sacraments*, London: Burns and Oates, p. 89.

6

Joy bears fruit (1): Ordination

Joyless debates

At various points throughout this book, the need for a fuller exploration of ordination has been apparent. One important dimension of confirmation, for example, was seen to be the relationship it established between the candidate and the bishop – making clear that being Christian is about membership of a people whose unity stretches across time and space, somehow symbolized and made real in the person of the bishop. Controversy over the eucharist and reconciliation has frequently involved sharp differences as to what ordained ministers are understood to be doing in them. Christianity is seldom consistently less joyful than in debates about the meaning of ordination. In this chapter, we will set out a vision of what ordination is which takes serious account of the points of pain, and does its best to heal them.

Why do Christians fight about ordination? Out of a wide range of possibilities, four principal areas suggest themselves.

First, there is the issue of sacerdotalism. By this we mean to indicate the classic Protestant rejection of what Luther and Calvin saw as the Roman Catholic understanding of ordination. Allegedly, this saw the ordained as somehow empowered to mediate between human beings and God. Salvation was dependent on the actions of the clergy, in their power to make present and offer the body and blood of Christ in the eucharist, or to pronounce the effective words of absolution in reconciliation. Christians needed priests to say the 'magic words' and perform the rites which alone could bring salvation. Reformers like Luther and Calvin believed this offended against the heart of the gospel: that Jesus' sacrifice had done away with the need for all other mediators. The Protestant stance is that Christians don't need priests to approach the distant Holy One on their behalf. Rather, every baptized person *is* a priest as Jesus lives within them, and shares with them his own relationship to his Father. This is the central Reformation doctrine of 'the priesthood of all believers'. Of course, certain baptized people are subsequently called to the ministry of preaching, teaching, pastoral care and administration of the sacraments: Reformed churches still have an ordained ministry. However, it in no sense mediated between humanity and God, and was certainly not to be considered as a special priesthood. Most Reformed churches dropped the word 'priest' as a description for their ordained ministers; Anglicans retained it, but even today are frequently anxious to emphasize that it has no sacerdotal implications.

A second, and closely related, reason why ordination seems chronically controversial is the issue of clericalism. Even the most Protestant and least sacerdotal views of ordination can still be deeply clericalist, insofar as they treat the ordained as a separate and superior caste of Christians to whom all others must defer. Clericalism is notoriously difficult to expunge, and arguably present in the very roots of this sacrament. Even the word 'ordination' derives from practices of power and status in ancient Rome, denoting the rite of admission to an 'order' in political society such as the senate or the judiciary. Ordination was admission to the exercise of the powers belonging to that order. Similarly, ordained Christian ministers have also been seen as vested with power: 'magical' power in the sacraments, or power to teach and discipline and order the life of the Church. Their supreme power, perhaps, has been in the sense that they are somehow closer to God than all other believers (an impression deliberately reinforced by compulsory clerical celibacy in the Roman tradition for most of the second millennium). Thus it has seemed natural to many in the Church (Roman and Reformed, lay and ordained) that authority belongs to the clergy, and that the role of the laity is to believe and do as they are told. Unsurprisingly, this has always bred resentment. Today, with the triumph of a democratic egalitarian spirit across western culture and an increasingly educated laity, such 'clericalism' is under pressure as never before. The scandal of clerical sexual abuse might sound its terrible final death knell – and yet the response to that scandal has shown that clericalism dies hard.

A third reason why discussion of ordination is so joyless is that it frequently seems to be a principal stumbling block in ecumenical dialogue. We have already seen some of the tensions between Roman Catholic and Protestant understandings of ordained ministry, but these are not the only problems. The Church of England, for instance, recognizes the German Lutheran and Reformed churches as sharing exactly the same faith as Anglicans, and being fully apostolic and catholic churches. However, it refuses to take the logical next step of allowing their ordained ministers to function interchangeably with Anglican clergy.[58]

58 For both the recognition and the refusal, see *The Meissen Agreement*, The Council of Christian Unity of the General Synod of the Church of England, Occasional Paper No. 2, 1988.

If such a minister wanted to become the parish priest in an Anglican parish, he or she would need to be re-ordained (or strictly speaking, ordained for the first time) by an Anglican bishop. This is because the German churches do not have an unbroken line of episcopal succession from apostolic times, and are not persuaded that they need one. Therefore, the Church of England treats them as if there is after all something lacking in their catholicity and apostolicity. This is sad enough. However, it is also hard to avoid the rather distasteful impression of a game of 'my church, my ordination is better than yours'. The game seems chiefly of interest to those with a special interest in clerical status: the clergy.

And lastly, of course, there is the ordination of women. After the *Final Report* of ARCIC-1 in 1981, many believed that full union between Rome and Canterbury was just around the corner. The ordination of women by Anglicans has been perhaps the principal factor in delaying that happy dawn for many years to come. The Roman Catholic Church and the Orthodox (and some Anglicans) are clear that, in their view, women simply cannot be ordained. It is not just that the church has never ordained women, and therefore has no authority to do so now. Rather, something about ordination means that it is an intrinsically male affair, and the Anglican decision to ignore this has allegedly definitively established that tradition as a Protestant sect. Of course, the Roman tradition is not at peace with itself in this view, however: there are many, many Roman Catholics wholly in favour of the ordination of women. This is just one example of how disputes about ordination cause bitter division not only between but within churches.

Sacerdotalism, clericalism, ecclesiastical one-upmanship, and gender: these are the sharp pressure points which drain joy from the theology of ordination.[59] How might we best respond?

A positive vision

In this section, we seek to set out our own vision of what ordination is about. It owes much to the western Catholic tradition of thinking about the sacrament, but neither Rome nor Canterbury would applaud it in all respects. It is offered not as an exposition of what either tradition thinks, but as an immodest suggestion as to what they *should* think.

The starting point is that Christianity is above all a sharing in joy: participation in a new common life breathed by Jesus in the Spirit, in which all the barriers which hold people apart from each other are broken down. Divisions of race, religion, wealth, power, sex, even the supreme division of death, are put aside. People who were locked into themselves, and into relationships with others characterized by competition, fear and hostility are instead freed to become bearers of joy to each other. Crucially, this means that Christianity is *not*, first and foremost, a message, a set of propositions or of moral rules. It is a people. Michael Ramsey used to say that the unity of Christians was fundamentally that of 'a new race'.[60]

This is why the Gospels record that one of Jesus' first public acts was to summon twelve apostles. The number is not arbitrary: twelve were called because twelve tribes had made up Israel in the beginning. Sin and death had taken

59 One important question which we do not address at all here – for reasons of space – is the theology of the diaconate.

60 Arthur Michael Ramsey, 1936, *The Gospel and the Catholic Church*, London: SPCK, 1990, p. 49.

their toll; some tribes had fallen by the wayside or ceased to be, but Jesus' mission was the restoration of Israel. Just as he had re-enacted through baptism in the Jordan the wandering Hebrews' entrance to the promised land, so he now symbolically refashioned Israel under the leadership of the Twelve. That is one reason why it is so important for St Luke that when Judas falls away, the number is promptly made up with the calling of Matthias. Jesus did not come to save individuals, but to raise up a people.

Strikingly, however, the Twelve soon fade from view after Easter. Paul cites them as among the first witnesses of the resurrection (1 Corinthians 15.3), but they do not occupy any significant place in his thought. What they signified, though, most certainly does. We have already encountered Paul's doctrine of the Church as 'the body of Christ': as a web of relationships in which every person is empowered by the Spirit of Jesus to awaken and enliven joy in every other person. To be Christian is to be someone through whom, in whom, by whom Jesus Christ is reaching out to rejoice with others. (This, to anticipate, should rule out any view of ordination which reduces most Christians to being passive recipients of others' agency.)

The Pauline idea of the body of Christ undergoes an interesting development (strikingly parallel to that traceable in Johannine Christianity, reading John's Gospel and the three letters of John).[61] In 1 Corinthians 12, all of Paul's emphasis falls upon the mutual enlivening which happens in the body. He is, as yet, relatively uninterested in the question of how this common life is actually held together. Unity is crucial to him,

---

61 The story of the Johannine community is plausibly reconstructed in Raymond E. Brown, 1979, *The Community of the Beloved Disciple: The Life, Loves and Hates of an Individual Church in New Testament Times*, London: Geoffrey Chapman.

but how unity is sustained does not yet preoccupy him. By the time he – or perhaps a disciple – writes to the Ephesians, however, things have changed. The intervening years have shown that the body simply will not hold together without structures and people charged with helping it do so. The common life is vulnerable, easily 'tossed to and fro and blown about by every wind of doctrine, by people's trickery, by their craftiness in deceitful scheming' (Ephesians 4.14). So 'Paul' places greater emphasis than before on what we might call 'bonds of unity': the apostles and their teaching as the foundation of the Church (2.20) and ministries which hold the Church to that foundation: 'apostles, prophets, evangelists, pastors and teachers' (4.11). These ministries are what 'Paul' has in mind when he refers to the 'ligaments' by which the whole body is joined and knitted together (4.16). They help secure the Church in Christ, and hold its common life together.

Ephesians then, along with the Pastoral Epistles and the Johannine correspondence, shows the later New Testament's increased focus on the structures which the Church needs to hold together and flourish. Of necessity, this focus developed in the course of the first three Christian centuries. For, Jesus and Christianity proved a remarkably successful 'brand' and soon there were many – very diverse – teachings and practices keen to present themselves as the genuine article. How was a would-be Christian in second-century Gaul, for instance, to know which of the many teachings on offer really was the gospel first proclaimed by the Twelve? Which community really was the common life created by Jesus and living in his power?

A second-century Gaulish bishop, Irenaeus of Lyons, offered the most historically influential answer to such questions. Confronted by those claiming to have inherited secret teaching passed down from Jesus, he challenged their credentials. Where have they come from? What continuity do they, or their teachings, possess with the apostles? They have no authority but their own. Irenaeus, and his fellow 'Catholic' bishops, by contrast could trace a line of succession back to the earliest times. The continuity of personnel represented by the bishop served as a guarantee that in his company, and his alone, the gospel was truly preached and lived: 'we are in a position to reckon up those who were by the apostles appointed bishops in the churches and (to demonstrate) the successions of those men to our own times; those who neither taught nor knew of anything like what these heretics rave about'.[62] Here, Irenaeus articulates a consistent, central theme of Patristic theology: if you want to be part of the true Church, stay faithful to a bishop who stands in succession from and communion with the bishops of the Church across time and space.

It is tempting to bewail this as a lapse from the earliest New Testament vision, with its relative lack of interest in bishops and total lack of interest in their succession. One powerful telling of the tale sees a decline from the Church as the Spirit-filled new creation to the Church understood in legalistic, institutional terms. However, it is just as plausible (and indeed fairer) to suggest that what Irenaeus is doing is maintaining Jesus and Paul's emphasis that salvation is truly social. Being Christian is about sharing a common life. You belong to a bishop not merely because the bishop is the guarantor of correct teaching, as if doctrine was all that mattered. Irenaeus, after all, like most Fathers, abominated schism even if the schismatics were perfectly orthodox doctrinally. You belong to a bishop, rather, because relationships matter; because what is adhered to is not merely doctrine, but the new race. That race identifies

62 Irenaeus, *Adversus Haereses*, 3.3.1.

itself, in part, through relationship with the central figure of the bishop. Through belonging with this person, they know they belong with the people of God throughout time and space.

This is the incarnational principle at work once again. In Christianity, inward and spiritual truths seek outward and visible reality. The spiritual unity of God's people is given outward, bodily expression through a bishop standing in succession from other bishops. Equally, the very act by which he became a bishop also has its outward and visible sign. A bishop is not a bishop until other bishops have physically laid their hands upon him. One reason why this laying on of hands is essential – quite apart from its distinguished biblical pedigree as a sign of commissioning – is that it serves as the bodily expression of the inward reality celebrated. The unity we share is one of people who can touch each other, before it is one of beliefs or morals.

At one level, the bishop testifies to all this simply by virtue of having been ordained. Before the bishop says or does anything, his ordination makes him as it were a signpost whereby his local church knows itself as sharing in the great Church spread across time and space. He is this signpost even if a bad bishop in every other way. However, the real purpose of ordination is not merely to produce mute signposts. Rather, ordination makes people around whom the common life of the Church is meant to flourish, knowing itself for what it truly is: a sharing in the joy of Jesus. They are commissioned not only to symbolize the knitting of the local and contemporary into the great communion of saints, but to be ways in which that knitting happens, in which individuals and communities come to live ever more deeply in Jesus. They are symbols which help to bring about what they symbolize – in Austin Farrer's phrase, 'walking sacraments'.[63]

The ordained exist to help the Church to be the Church – to enable the joy of Jesus to flow ever more freely through ever more lives. The basic ways in which they do this include prayer, preaching and teaching, pastoral care and administration of the sacraments. It is not that only the ordained can do these things, still less that ordination confers quasi-magical power to perform them. Even in sacramental ministry, where the latter error has a powerful shelf-life, no one disputes that laypeople can perform the most potent sacramental act of all: baptism. There is nothing in the nature of things which means a layperson cannot preach, teach, exercise pastoral care or even (exceptionally) preside at the eucharist.[64] However, all these things belong most naturally with the ordained ministry, as the characteristic ways in which it fulfils its purpose of knitting people into the joy of Jesus. Ordination is not about receiving magic powers, but embarking on a life dedicated to these particular tasks and the one controlling vocation to help the Church share ever more deeply in the joy of Jesus.

In some ways, then, ordination is quite terrifying. 'Who is sufficient for these things?', St Paul said of his own apostolic ministry (2 Corinthians 2.16). The ordained are to be people around whom, through whom, joy happens. People like

---

63 The title of one of Farrer's most famous sermons, reproduced in Ann Loades and Robert MacSwain, eds, 2006, *The Truth-Seeking Heart: Austin Farrer and his Writings*, Norwich: Canterbury Press, pp. 138–42.

64 Lay presidency at the eucharist is of course especially controversial. Official Roman Catholic teaching would never countenance it, nor does current Anglican canon law. However, many Anglicans could be persuaded if the circumstances were truly exceptional – and some would not need much persuasion.

Augustine understood the stark gap between that vocation, and what they actually were – and hence were only dragged unwillingly to be ordained. There is probably a degree of hagiography in many such tales, but they do bring home the important point that what is asked of the ordained is beyond them. So it is of the utmost importance that ordination is understood not merely as the Church charging particular people with this great responsibility. To understand ordination as a sacrament is to say that in the Church's act, Jesus himself is active. Through the laying on of hands and the prayers of the Church, Jesus takes a human person and makes them one of his ways into the world. That person remains a sinner, but when he prays, preaches and administers the sacraments, ordination means that ultimately it is not him who acts. Rather, Jesus acts in him and through him. In his defence of the reality of Donatist baptisms, Augustine developed a principle which became central for all Catholic theology: that the unworthiness of the human minister does not impede the grace of the sacrament. 'Christ's gift is not thereby profaned: what flows through him keeps its purity, and what passes through him remains clear and reaches the fertile earth . . . The spiritual power of the sacrament is indeed comparable to light: those to be enlightened receive it in its purity, and if it should pass through defiled beings, it is not itself defiled.'[65]

One way Catholic theology has articulated this is by saying that ordination impresses a person with the sacramental 'character' of Christ. That is to say, the ordained person is not just a chosen representative of the Church, mandated to perform certain functions on behalf of the whole body (as the Reformation doctrine of the priesthood of all believers

65 Augustine, *Homilies on John* 5.15.

can suggest). Rather, Jesus has laid hold of the ordained person in such a way as to make their actions his own actions. Without ceasing to be a member of the Church, the ordained person is set in a distinctive relationship to other believers. He is the one through whom Jesus knits others into his joy. If the Church is continually renewed through Jesus' leaping out of himself in joy, then the ordained and their actions are how that leap takes place – how joy happens. Of course, as we have argued previously in relation to baptism, Jesus can act independently of and beyond his ordained ministry. Nevertheless, this is how he promised to do so and where he can be reliably encountered: 'Jesus said to them again, "Peace be with you. As the Father has sent me, so I send you." When he had said this, he breathed on them and said to them, "Receive the Holy Spirit. If you forgive the sins of any, they are forgiven; if you retain the sins of any, they are retained"' (John 20.21–23, a key text in many ordination rites).

Is all this inevitably sacerdotal or clericalizing? Does it offend against the principle that all Christians share immediately in the joy of Jesus, and that after Easter there is no need for other mediators between humans and God, or for their rituals? Does it conceive the ordained as a separate and superior class of Christian, or imply an authoritarian church with the laity reduced to passive dependence upon and obedience to the ordained?

On sacerdotalism, the answer must be nuanced. In one sense, this understanding of ordination does make the existence of the Church dependent upon the ordained ministry. The latter indeed plays a mediating role in salvation, insofar as the risen Jesus wills to share his joy through ordinary human actions. It might help to imagine a deep pool, supplied by underwater springs. Viewed one way, those springs are simply part of the pool. Viewed differently, with equal truth, they are the ways in which the pool is replenished, without which it dries up. From one angle, they are simply the point of entry for water into the pool and not in themselves the source of its life; from another, they are the way the water has 'chosen' to arrive and are essential to the pool's flourishing. The ordained bear a similar relationship to the Church. It is true to say that they are simply part of the common life, like any other believer. It is equally true to say that they have become the way joy chooses to give itself to the Church. They do indeed mediate salvation – because the one Mediator chooses to give himself through them. They do not compete with his action, but are the form of that action. So, yes: this is a sacerdotal view.

However, it is emphatically not clericalist. One of the great strengths of the theology advocated here is that it allows one to face with utter clarity the catastrophic failure of so many clergy to live up to their vocation, and yet not to despair. In ordination Jesus lays hold of people in such a way that even despite themselves their actions will be his actions. He is the true minister behind all their ministry. It is of course to be hoped that people will respond to the greatness of the gift and call given in ordination, but (as with baptism) Jesus' action in a sacrament is not ultimately dependent upon the quality of our response to it. Such a theology allows clergy to be weak, sinful people – and is an effective remedy against all fantasy which sees them otherwise.

Furthermore, if Jesus works through the ordained minister, his working now will be continuous with his working in the incarnation. While there is certainly authority here – God is truly at work – it is not a worldly authority of domination and violence. Jesus did not intimidate, manipulate or control others. Joy does not force, but sets people free. If the ordained are truly bearers of the ongoing ministry of Jesus, then their ministry will look like his does. It will have no other power than love, and be beautifully free of concerns about ego and status: 'The kings of the Gentiles lord it over them; and those in authority over them are called benefactors. But not so with you; rather the greatest among you must become like the youngest, and the leader like one who serves . . . I am among you as one who serves' (Luke 22.25–26, 27b). That so much in church culture betrays this vision says less about flaws in the theology of ordination than it does about the deep-seated flaw in our natures.

Difficult questions for a positive vision

We have so far begged two difficult questions which must now be faced. First, in taking our cue in the theology of ordination from Irenaeus, we followed his lead in speaking much about the importance of bishops and continuous episcopal succession from apostolic times.[66] Many churches today lack either one or both. Does this matter at all, and how should we view the ordained ministry of such churches? Equally, there are churches which clearly have people preaching, pastoring and administering sacraments who would not begin to conceptualize the theology of ordination (if they even spoke in such terms) in the way done here. What are we to make of them? Is a Baptist pastor the same thing as a Catholic priest?

---

66 In contemporary ecumenical theology, the term 'apostolic succession' is quite properly used in a broad sense to describe all the ways in which a church may maintain continuity with the apostles. For convenience, however, we will use it in an older and narrower sense to designate an unbroken chain of episcopal consecrations believed traceable to the apostles and Jesus. In this sense, Roman Catholics, Orthodox and Anglicans believe themselves to possess 'the apostolic succession' (Rome and the Orthodox refuting the Anglican claim).

Second, the official Catholic and Orthodox position (to which the vision outlined in the last section owes much) assumes that the ordained person must be male. For these churches, maleness is intrinsic to the mediatory role played by the ordained. Is there anything to that case, and what response might be made to it?

The first question first. According to contemporary Roman Catholic doctrine, the fullness of the sacrament of ordination is conferred only upon bishops. They are the ones who have received from Jesus, acting through his apostles and their successors, the gift of mediating his joy to the Church; they are the ones through whom he promises to be active in renewing his people. They share this gift with their presbyters (or priests), but the latter are always utterly dependent on the bishop as the source of their ministry. Accordingly, presbyters never ordain. They may join with the bishop as he lays hands on new ministers, as a sign of their belonging with him, but it is the bishop's action alone which creates a new ordained ministry. Neither Roman doctrine nor practice was utterly unambiguous on this point until as late as the Second Vatican Council (1962–65), but that Council stated the position with complete clarity.[67]

The logic of it is that an unbroken chain of episcopal succession from the apostles is essential to there being any ordained ministry today, and hence to the Church's contemporary existence. Communities which lack such succession may be full of many virtues and gifts, but lack the ordained ministry through which Jesus promised to be present to sustain and renew his people. For that reason,

67 Walter M. Abbot, ed., 1966, *Documents of Vatican II*, London and Dublin: Geoffrey Chapman, *Lumen Gentium*, p. 39, para. 20.

as we observed when dealing with the eucharist, Rome strictly speaking does not recognize such communities as 'the Church' but rather as 'ecclesial communities'. Whatever good they possess cries out for completion – like Donatist baptism – in reintegration with the Catholic Church. Their clergy may be wonderful Christians whose work has been truly blessed by God, but they are not truly ordained. They have not been sacramentally impressed with the character of Jesus, and therefore they must be 're-ordained' (more accurately, ordained for the first time) before they could serve as Catholic priests. Thus, for example, those Anglican clergy who have joined the recently established Ordinariate have had to receive the sacrament of ordination as if it were for the first time.

If this offends Anglicans, they should consider that other churches frequently hear them as saying something rather similar. Only one strand within Anglicanism shares the Roman view that the bishop alone shares fully in the apostolic ministry, and consequently that apostolic succession in episcopal ministry is essential to the Church (while simultaneously denying, of course, Rome's view that Anglicanism lacks such succession). However, a much broader Anglican trend is to insist upon the necessity of episcopal succession while remaining coy about the rationale (for instance, in the Church of England's dealings with the German Lutheran and Reformed churches). This is not merely a matter of seeking assurance that any German Protestant minister seeking to work in the Church of England will accept the authority of the diocesan bishop. That could be addressed by the quite different and non-sacramental process of licensing, which happens at the beginning of all new ministries in the Church of England. That Anglicans insist rather upon ordination implies that something is lacking in the 'ordinations' already received, and that others' ministries are not really so catholic and apostolic as once acknowledged. What is lacking is ordination by a bishop who stands in an unbroken chain of episcopal succession from apostolic times: the Roman Catholic position without the Roman Catholic theology to justify it.

A fundamental problem for both stances is that the evidence of the New Testament and the early Church is too slight to bear the weight placed upon it. Certainly, by the middle of the second century there was a broad pattern emerging of churches headed by bishops claiming succession from the apostles. However, to say that in all cases such a succession actually existed – in the strict sense of a chain of ordinations stretching back to the Twelve and to Jesus – goes well beyond what can be plausibly established. As already observed, the Twelve soon disappear from view in the New Testament. We have no record of their undertaking wide missionary journeys, ordaining successors as they went. It is simply impossible to show that all (even most) ordained ministry in the second century could trace itself back to apostolic ordination. Logically, therefore, the same holds true today.[68]

Moreover, at various stages in church history, presbyters have clearly been considered capable of ordaining their successors. It was always thought important that this was done under episcopal authority, but this was frequently justified as a matter of good discipline rather than of the presbyterate

68 Raymond E. Brown, 1971, *Priest and Bishop: Biblical Reflections*, London, Dublin, Melbourne: Geoffrey Chapman, pp. 51–5.

being essentially incapable of ordaining.[69] That church life shapes itself around a bishop, and that ordaining normally falls to the bishop, does not mean that in exceptional circumstances (and throughout history, not always that exceptional) the continuity of ordained ministry might not be mediated through the actions of the presbyterate.

Both considerations tell against the Orthodox, Roman Catholic and Anglican practice of treating churches which do not claim an unbroken chain of episcopal consecration from the apostles as somehow lacking in apostolicity and catholicity. A better policy might be to ask what such churches think they are doing when they ordain people. Are they constituting people as a visible bond of the unity of the communion of saints spread throughout time and space? Do they believe that in that action Jesus lays hold of these people in such a way that their ministry becomes the form of his ministry – that they become reliable springs through whom the joy of Jesus flows into the Church? If the answer to both questions is yes, then there should be no problem embracing their ministers as catholic and apostolic in exactly the same sense as Anglicans, Romans and Orthodox ministers – and accordingly no suggestion of 're-ordination'.

What though when the answer to those questions is not clear? What about a Baptist pastor who might not even think in terms of having been ordained, and certainly not of that ordination expressing and sustaining the unity of

69 See T. G. Jalland, 1946, 'The Doctrine of the Parity of Ministers', in Kenneth Kirk, ed., *The Apostolic Ministry: Essays on the History and Doctrine of Episcopacy*, London: Hodder and Stoughton, pp. 305–49. Like all the essayists in this volume, Jalland was convinced that the episcopate alone is the true apostolic ministry – but he was a rigorously honest historian who acknowledged how much in the history of doctrine and practice told against this view.

the communion of saints or conferring the sacramental character of Jesus? Of course such a pastor and his church may be deeply catholic and apostolic, in the sense that their corporate life may be radiant with the joy of Jesus. As one recent (Anglican!) writer has put it, 'a church is catholic, not through legislative or institutional pedigree, but because it demonstrates . . . Christlike qualities and concerns'.[70] Churches which are quite confident of their apostolic succession in the ministry may indeed have much to learn from those quite uninterested in such things.

However, we should not be too quickly dismissive of 'institutional pedigree'. What the phrase denotes is whether or not a church has organized itself so as to give expression to great spiritual truths. A church which is quite unbothered about succession in ordained ministry suggests a church quite unbothered about belonging visibly within the great Church across time and space, and quite unbothered as to the source of whatever authority its ministers possess. Succession in the ministry is not the most important thing in a church, but nor is it irrelevant if that church wants to signify the fact that it is part of the communion of saints and that its life comes to it from Jesus alone. As another great Anglican theologian wrote in a classic statement of the incarnational principle: 'spirit corresponds with body, as body with spirit; and those who have tried to cut loose from what seemed to them merely outward, find more and more, in fact, that in losing reality of body they have been losing reality of spirit too'.[71]

70 Robin Greenwood, 1994, *Transforming Priesthood: A New Theology of Mission and Ministry*, London: SPCK, p. 130.

71 R. C. Moberly, 1899, *Ministerial Priesthood: Chapters (Preliminary to a Study of the Ordinal) On the Rationale and the Meaning of Christian Priesthood, with an Appendix upon Roman Catholic Criticism of Anglican Orders*, London: John Murray, p. 55.

So that Baptist pastor is in a rather different position than, say, the Methodist presbyter. Wonderful, gifted and blessed as their ministry may be, their commissioning did not mean what ordination does. Were they to seek to be what an ordained priest is, they would need to be ordained.

What of the ordination of women? Is that another example of those who cut loose from what seems merely outward – a restriction on the gender of candidates for ordination – in fact losing inner reality too? Can you ordain women without losing what ordination is about? The Roman Catholic Church, Orthodoxy and some Anglicans take the view that you cannot. For some the argument is simply that from tradition and authority: the Church has never done this, therefore it should never be done – at least, not until the highest authority possible (Pope or Ecumenical Council) has said so. That argument should not detain us here, though every stage of it is open to challenge.[72] More relevant in a book about sacraments is the stronger version of the refusal: that the tradition has a rationale which means that no authority *could* reverse it. As it was offensively but clearly stated by one opponent, you could no more ordain a woman than you could ordain a potato.[73] Something in the nature of the sacrament, and the nature of women, rules it

72 See, among many useful texts, Paul Avis, 1997, *Anglican Orders and the Ordination of Women*, London: Darton, Longman and Todd; and McAdoo, Henry, 1997, *Anglicans, Tradition and the Ordination of Women*, Norwich: Canterbury Press.

73 The remark is widely attributed to Graham Leonard, an Anglican bishop who converted to Roman Catholicism in part because of his opposition to women's ordination. I have been unable to trace a precise reference for it.

out. This is the official position of the Roman Catholic Church.[74]

The argument is rooted in the fact that Jesus himself was male, and chose only males to be his apostles. It goes on to claim that this was not an accident: that what Jesus did, and what he still does through the apostles and their successors, requires him to be male. One clue to understanding this might be to think back to the chapter on the eucharist, where we discussed the sacrifice of Jesus on the cross. Jesus poured himself out into the darkness of sin and death to bring life. His total self-expenditure was to have, as it were, a fertilizing effect in the sterile darkness of death, to generate and quicken life where there was none. For official Roman Catholic teaching, such generativity is intrinsically male. This view is based, in part, on the ancient and medieval theory of reproduction which saw the male seed as the essentially active element in procreation. The womb was receptive, responding to the male initiative – but the male was the potent source. Similarly, in Roman Catholic ecclesiology, the Church tends to be imagined as female, waiting on the quickening gift of life from Jesus. Jesus has willed that this quickening gift should come through the apostolic ministry, which he has made to be the potent source of the Church's life. Tellingly, the Second Vatican Council described that ministry's role as one of 'transmitting the apostolic seed'.[75] Given that this is the inner spiritual reality, it is given best bodily expression by the ordained ministry being male. (One might also argue that it is given best expression by the laity

74 Sacred Congregation for the Doctrine of the Faith, 1976, *Inter Insigniores: Declaration on the Admission of Women to the Ministerial Priesthood.*

75 *Lumen Gentium*, para. 20, p. 39.

being purely passive, docile recipients of ordained action . . . and, incidentally, female.)

As with some teaching on apostolic succession, it is facts which tell most strongly against all this. Just as the idea that all ordained ministry in the Church can trace itself directly to the apostles is deeply implausible, so we know that the theory of reproduction upon which this teaching rests is inaccurate. The male seed is not the only potent source of new life: the female (in a different way) is just as active in procreation as the male. Take the ancient theory of reproduction away, and the activity of Jesus no longer seems essentially male. One might even start to rejoice in the recognition made by medievals such as Julian of Norwich that Jesus' creative act on the cross could be equally well understood through classically female actions such as childbirth.[76] One can imagine Jesus seeding the world with new life; one can imagine his death agonies as the birthpangs of a new world. Neither approach is self-evidently a better way than the other.

Jesus had to be either male or female. Most humans are one or the other (though significantly not all – the definition and prevalence of 'intersex' conditions is contested, but their existence casts doubt on a too crudely binary distinction of genders). We might even allow that it was no accident that he was male, that in the deep plan of God his maleness somehow made sense. However, one of the constant themes of this book has been that through Easter and Pentecost, Jesus Christ has become more than the individual human being who walked around Galilee and Jerusalem. He is no longer a private person. Rather his life ripples through billions of other lives, making them

76 Julian of Norwich, *Showings*, Ch. 60.

his own. All lives become capable of bearing Jesus, being the way in which Jesus works. As Paul said: 'As many of you as were baptized into Christ have clothed yourselves with Christ. There is no longer Jew or Greek, there is no longer slave or free, there is no longer male and female; for all of you are one in Christ Jesus' (Galatians 3.27–28). If women can be baptized, women can be ordained – because to be baptized is to be incorporated in Jesus.

Quoting Paul, however, invites a different objection to the ordination of women. Didn't Paul also say, 'Let a woman learn in silence with full submission. I permit no woman to teach or to have authority over a man; she is to keep silent. For Adam was formed first, then Eve; and Adam was not deceived, but the woman was deceived and became a transgressor' (1 Timothy 2.11–14)? Actually Paul probably did not say this: most scholars don't think he wrote 1 Timothy. But whoever wrote it, the more important point is that it is a terrible argument. What does the writer mean by saying that Adam was not deceived? Is he (one strongly suspects a 'he'!) suggesting that the male is somehow less guilty of sin than the female? Or can we – after Darwin – make arguments based on Adam's supposed chronological priority over Eve? This argument, were it not contained in Scripture, would be laughed out of court in an instant. Because it *is* contained in Scripture, some Christians feel obliged to take it seriously. This is not a book about biblical authority, and therefore we cannot address that problem adequately. Suffice it to say that such believers are logically also obliged to believe that God commanded genocide (1 Samuel 15.3), and that Cretans 'are always liars, vicious brutes, lazy gluttons' (Titus 1.12). (Those of them who are English Anglicans also need to think carefully about how they regard their Supreme Governor, who happens to be a woman.)

There is nothing in the nature of things which makes it impossible for women to be ordained. The sacramental representation of Christ does not require one to be male, because there is nothing exclusively male about what Jesus does or even, after Easter, about who Jesus is. The exercise of authority does not require one to be male unless one is committed to a particular theory of the inerrancy of Scripture in all its parts. Even then, one would still be faced with challenging questions about what kind of authority it is assumed is being conferred in ordination. The joyful authority of Jesus did not seem to have much to do with reducing others to silent submission. There simply is no strong theological argument against ordaining women. When the traditional refusal is quizzed it is shown to rest on deeply unreasonable foundations, and then one is left simply with the argument that it has never been done before. Even if that is so (a moot point), that it can never be done does not follow.

A final thought. Could the vision which sees the ordained priesthood as essentially male, fertilizing the Church with apostolic seed, be part of the reason why in the Roman tradition for the best part of a millennium celibacy has been considered mandatory for clergy (albeit a rule often hotly disputed or honoured in the breach)? There are many reasons for clerical celibacy, of course, not least the church's historic denigration of human sexuality as somehow alien to the truly Christian life. But another has been quite the reverse: an instinct that there is a curious closeness between the sacrament of marriage and that of ordination. The ordained are married to the Church. Their maleness finds expression not through sex but through a radically different, yet radically similar, self-giving to Jesus and his people. The married are given to each other: a similar love, but lived out in a different way, bearing different fruit. One doesn't have to be Roman Catholic, or take the further step of believing the two sacraments to be mutually exclusive, to think there might be something in the intuition of their deep kinship. And so we turn to the theology of marriage.

FOR DISCUSSION

- What does ordination mean in your church?
- Would it matter – for good or ill – if someone other than an ordained minister presided at the eucharist? Why?
- Is it possible to have a sacerdotal understanding of ordination which is not also clericalist?
- What difference do you see between a Baptist pastor and a Catholic priest?
- What might the value of clerical celibacy be?

FOR REFLECTION

> You did not choose me but I chose you. And I appointed you to go and bear fruit, fruit that will last . . .
> *John 15.16*

> The same power of the word also makes the priest revered and honourable, separated from community with the general public by the new quality given by the blessing. Yesterday, he was one of the crowd, one of the people: he is suddenly made into a leader, a president, a teacher of religion, a guide into hidden mysteries: and he performs these functions without being changed in

any way in body or in form. He continues to be the same as before to all appearance; but he is transformed to a higher state in respect of his invisible soul by an invisible power and grace.
Gregory of Nyssa[77]

As for the proud minister, he is to be ranked with the devil. Christ's gift is not thereby profaned: what flows through him keeps its purity, and what passes through him remains clear and reaches the fertile earth . . . The spiritual power of the sacrament is indeed comparable to light: those to be enlightened receive it in its purity, and if it should pass through defiled beings, it is not itself defiled.
Augustine of Hippo[78]

The power of the ministry of God translateth out of darkness into glory, it raiseth men from the earth and bringeth God himself down from heaven, by blessing visible elements it maketh them invisible grace, it giveth daily the Holy Ghost, it hath to dispose of that flesh which was given for the life of the world and that blood which was poured out to redeem souls, when it poureth malediction on the heads of the wicked they perish, when it revoketh the same they revive. O wretched blindness if we admire not so great power, more wretched if we consider it aright and notwithstanding imagine that any but God can bestow it!
Richard Hooker[79]

77 Gregory of Nyssa, 'On the Baptism of Christ'.
78 Augustine, *Homilies on John*, 5,15.
79 Richard Hooker, *Laws of Ecclesiastical Polity*, Book V: 77,2.

Aaron

Holinesse on the head,
Light and perfections on the breast,
Harmonious bells below, raising the dead
To leade them unto life and rest.
Thus are true Aarons drest.

Profanenesse in my head,
Defects and darknesse in my breast,
A noise of passions ringing me for dead
Unto a place where is no rest.
Poore priest thus am I drest.

Onely another head
I have, another heart and breast,
Another musick, making live not dead,
Without whom I could have no rest:
In him I am well drest.

Christ is my onely head,
My alone onely heart and breast,
My onely musick, striking me ev'n dead;
That to the old man I may rest,
And be in him new drest.

So holy in my head,
Perfect and light in my deare breast,
My doctrine tun'd by Christ, (who is not dead,
But lives in me while I do rest)
Come people, Aaron's drest.

George Herbert

May your strength give us strength, may your faith give us faith, may your hope give us hope, may your love give us love . . .
Bruce Springsteen[80]

---

80 'Into the Fire', on the album *The Rising*, Columbia Records, 2002. Springsteen's song is not, it should be noted, about ordination!

7

Joy bears fruit (II): Marriage

A difficult history

Jesus likes weddings. That has to be the simplest meaning of the story of the wedding at Cana (John 2.1–11). It is not just weddings that he likes either, but wedding receptions. At Cana, when the wine ran out, Jesus produced something like one thousand bottles worth of the finest wine to keep the celebrations going. Bride and groom rejoice; friends, family and wider society rejoice with them, and at Cana we see that joy caught on the surge of divine joy which is Jesus, and carried by him to new heights.

Why does Jesus like weddings? For the same reasons, no doubt, as most people. Those reasons have not always been the same: weddings have often been as much (or more) about cementing political and economic family alliances as about love between man and woman. Beneath all the changing contexts, though, there is one abiding meaning. Marriage means the coming together of lives in hope for the future – hope characteristically realized in the creation of new life (even political and financial alliances need heirs). It is a great statement of faith in what one contemporary novelist has called 'the human thing', a 'yes' to the sense that we are summoned to contribute and belong to something greater than our own existence, to a collective story which is going somewhere.[81] At one level an arrangement for passing on genes effectively, at another marriage signifies the passionate desire and conviction that joy shall triumph over death.

Marriage is unique among the sacraments in that it long pre-dates Christianity, indeed written history. 'From the beginning of creation,' Jesus taught (echoing Genesis 1), 'God made them male and female. For this reason a man shall leave his father and mother and be joined to his wife, and the two shall become one flesh' (Mark 10.6–7). Jesus rejoices at Cana because, in marrying, that man and woman said yes to the human thing, and answered a call rooted deep in their nature. They did what they were created to do, and their Creator's joy resounded in theirs.

At which point, it is worth recalling that Jesus was in all probability *not* married. He rejoices with those who are, but Christianity could not sensibly teach that being married is somehow the only way to fulfil the human vocation. Arguably, the Cana story itself is intended to suggest that for all the joy of a wedding, we are called to something more wonderful still – that all human goods (the love of man and woman, true religion, wine) are but glimpses of the joyous glory which waits to be revealed. For the sake of that greater joy, very precious human ties might need to be set aside. Jesus told a man keen to follow him but keener still to obey the natural obligation and sacred command to bury his father: 'Let the dead bury their own dead; but as for you, go and proclaim the kingdom of God' (Luke 9.60). He praised those who made themselves eunuchs for the sake of that Kingdom (Matthew 9.12), and

---

81 Lionel Shriver, 2003, *We Need to Talk about Kevin*, London: Serpent's Tail, p. 27.

at one point apparently contrasted marriage unfavourably with celibacy: 'Those who belong to this age marry and are given in marriage; but those who are considered worthy of a place in that age and in the resurrection from the dead neither marry nor are given in marriage' (Luke 20.34–35 – more on this very important passage in the next chapter).

Nevertheless, marriage played a very important part in Jesus' thought and life. When the Pharisees challenged him as to why his disciples did not fast, his answer was revealing: 'The wedding guests cannot fast when the bridegroom is with them, can they?' (Mark 2.19). He seems here and elsewhere to have thought of himself as the Bridegroom of his people – a role traditionally occupied in Jewish thought by God himself (e.g. Ezekiel 16). In this light, Cana can be seen as the wedding feast not only for two villagers but as the inauguration of the long-awaited messianic wedding feast, when God would marry his people. All that follows is the working out of God's marriage vow, climaxing on the cross when Jesus spends himself utterly ('this is my body, given for you . . .') and cries, 'It is finished' – in Latin, *consummatus est.* The erotic resonances are plain, and have already been encountered in the previous chapter.

For his part, Paul has a complicated attitude to marriage. His earlier correspondence never gets beyond lukewarm endorsement: 'I wish that all were as I myself am (celibate) . . . But if they are not practising self-control, they should marry. For it is better to marry than to be aflame with passion' (1 Corinthians 7.7, 9). In fairness to Paul, at this stage he probably expected the imminent end of the world and marriage may therefore have seemed rather redundant. Had he envisaged centuries of church teaching being based upon his words, he may have written otherwise. But instead we have these words, which see marriage purely as a kind of safety valve through which humanity's sexual urges may be carefully channelled. He then adds a further caution: married people make second-rate disciples: 'The unmarried man is anxious about the affairs of the Lord, how to please the Lord; but the married man is anxious about the affairs of the world, how to please his wife, and his interests are divided . . .' (1 Corinthians 7.32–34). This chapter will argue that on both points he stands in need of correction.

If Paul wrote Ephesians, though, the picture is more positive. In the course of giving instruction on how husbands and wives should behave, the writer seems to stumble into greater realms of mystery as he contemplates marriage's true significance (Ephesians 5.21–33). Husbands should love their wives with utter devotion, because they have been made radically one with their wives. The wife is no possession or servant. Rather she is to the husband what the Church is to Christ – the one into whom his life is poured, the one suffused with his joy, the one without whom he can no longer be. Through the prism of marriage, the author glimpses the christological mystery we have emphasized repeatedly in this book: that after Easter and Pentecost, Jesus Christ is no longer merely a private individual but lives in and through his body, the disciples. He does not cease being himself, but is himself in and through all these others: 'and they will become one flesh . . . this is a great mystery, and I am applying it to Christ and the church'. The passage is not exactly a retraction of 1 Corinthians 7, but does see marriage as something rather better than a safety valve or a distraction.

Sadly, in Patristic theology the joy of Cana and the awe of Ephesians is almost wholly drowned by a chorus of anxiety and hostility towards human sexuality. Augustine's *Confessions* are especially instructive. It is just about possible to argue from them that Augustine was so struck by the beauty and joy for which we are destined that he merely wanted to prevent believers from becoming fixated on lesser joys. That certainly explains his caution about music in church, for example. With sex, however, the picture is different. His revulsion comes across clearly, and he seldom speaks of sexual desire even as a lesser good. He enjoyed sex – emphatically so – but regarded this as evidence of his base, animalistic nature from which he desperately sought redemption. Such is his self-disgust that one might think he was guilty of appalling sexual deviance. Yet the horror is actually directed against a loving, monogamous relationship from which was born a much-loved son. In Augustine's mind, the sexual element of this was terrible sin (abandoning his lover first for career and then for God, however, seems not to trouble him).[82] Later, this deep hostility towards all things sexual led Augustine to take the step – so fateful for subsequent western theology – of identifying intercourse as the mechanism through which the infection of original sin is passed.

Accordingly, for Augustine celibacy is the superior course for Christians. Like Paul, he acknowledges that some will not be able to control their sexual desire. Unlike Paul, however, he also realizes that history probably still has some considerable time to run, and that the species does need to propagate itself. So he considers marriage to be God's damage-limitation exercise for this unhappy state of affairs. Christians may marry, if they must, to contain sexual desire and to have children – but, as one commentator has said, for Augustine the ideal act of procreation

---

82 Of the many passages in *Confessions* which could be cited, see Book VI:20–26.

'would have all the passion of the act of artificial donor insemination'.[83]

So just what is wrong with sex? The clue is in that word 'passion'. Augustine is above all a theologian of desire; his writings burn with a fierce longing for God. But for him desire must be rightly ordered: aimed at the right object, pursued in the right way. If we are to be really human, free and happy, we must desire rightly – which means *rationally*. Reason tells us that God alone can satisfy the infinite desires of the human heart, so our desire should be for him alone. But sexual desire is unreasonable. With overwhelming power, it wrenches us from God and confuses everything. In its grip we behave wildly, our desires and bodies out of all control. Right desire degenerates into passion, the truly human into brutes. The actual act of intercourse, with all its messy abandon, illustrates the point perfectly. Augustine has been there, and shudders with disgust and fear.

Augustine speaks for great swathes of Christian antiquity. The consensus owes much to a whole melange of different philosophical and religious beliefs sweeping around the Mediterranean in the first four Christian centuries – from the sophisticated ideas of Plato and Plotinus, through religious movements like the Manichees (which Augustine once adhered to), to the myriad fantasies and speculations which came to shelter under the umbrella term 'Gnosticism'. But it would not be fair to say that all this is simply alien intrusion upon a more positive biblical tradition. Yes, there was the story of Cana, and in the Hebrew Scriptures the wonderfully erotic Song of Songs – a paean to sexual love. But there was also 1 Corinthians 7, or Revelation 14, which

83 Richard Holloway, 1992, *Anger, Sex, Doubt and Death*, London: SPCK, p. 54.

appears to suggest heaven will be populated only by those 'who have not defiled themselves with women, for they are virgins' (Revelation 14.4).[84] Equally, no careful reader of the Hebrew Scriptures could say those texts are wholly at peace with sexuality. Adam and Eve began in perfect bliss, but the very first consequence of their sin involved shame in their nakedness (Genesis 1.25; 2.7, 10): the beginning of angst about bodies and sexuality. It is also striking how frequently Israel's faithlessness and failure are depicted in ferociously sexual terms, almost pornographic in their intensity (Jeremiah 2.20–25; Ezekiel 16). Why should sex become the obvious metaphor for sin and ruin? Because long before Plato and Augustine, like nearly all human cultures the Jews sensed an ambivalence about their sexual nature – experiencing it both as blessing and as curse, and in both ways deeply charged with power.

Modern westerners are not so different. We consider ourselves infinitely more relaxed about sexuality, but there are signs that all is not well. Think of the staggering scale of sexual abuse, and of what it is like to be an abuser as well as a victim – many are both. Or of how a culture which prides itself on not being prudish is afflicted instead with mass addiction to pornography. It has been plausibly suggested that porn appeals to a deep-seated fear of real sex – true, vulnerable intimacy with another person and the loss of control which comes with that. And while we are all too ready to make the same charge against celibacy, there is something suspicious

84 It's not clear whether the author of Revelation thinks any women will be in heaven. His work provides several instances where modern translations of the Scriptures may get things seriously wrong by automatically adding the words 'and sisters' where the Greek has only 'brothers'!

in our almost total inability to see anything positive in that practice. Even sexual restraint is frequently pathologized, despite the negative consequences of undisciplined sex being in evidence all around. There is sufficient misery around contemporary sexuality to stop the wise from being too scornful of Augustine and his world.

Like Augustine, the men responsible for shaping the Church's sacramental theology well into the second millennium were celibate. With honourable exceptions (see for instance the words of Gregory Nazianzen cited at the end of this chapter) they shared his disdain for the whole business of marriage. Nevertheless, new humans and new Christians had to come from somewhere. Christians had to reproduce. How were they to do so in a way that was not sinful – or at least involved nothing more than the inescapable taint of Augustinian original sin? The eventual answer (which did not come till the eleventh century) was that marriage must be a sacrament. In it, Jesus would lay hold of believers' lives, including their sexual desires, and fill those desires with himself. Strengthened by this sacrament Christians could procreate without lust, the deranging passion that destroys union with God.

Arguably, this meant that at last the way was opened to seeing married Christians as more than second-class Christians. The celibate Church had finally, grudgingly, acknowledged that sexually active people could live truly holy lives. Consequently, marriages now came to be celebrated in church before a priest: prior to the eleventh century, there had been no required religious ritual (which might imply approval of sexual activity) for marriage at all. Of course, what must be ritualized in church can also be more effectively regulated, and the eleventh-century development can also be seen as marking a more determined policing of sexuality by the Church. At around the same time, for instance, the impetus towards mandatory clerical celibacy in the West was beginning to gather force. So the recognition of marriage as a sacrament had not dispelled the deep suspicion of sexuality. The Church was still a long way from Cana.

The Protestant Reformers denied that marriage was a sacrament. Yes, Jesus had esteemed marriage, but he had not laid down any particular way of marrying people, nor promised to act through the Church's action. For the Reformers, therefore, calling marriage a sacrament – as with anointing, confirmation, reconciliation and ordination before – was unjustified and unnecessary, tended to overstate the importance of the clergy through requiring their involvement, and needed pruning. It is important to note that the relegation of marriage from the rank of sacrament was therefore not due to a negative view of human sexuality. Luther, Calvin and Cranmer were all married themselves and determined to make the point that there was nothing superior about celibacy. That formed part of their bigger agenda of stripping the sacerdotal mystique from medieval Catholic priesthood, and asserting the priesthood of all believers. Indirectly, this paved the way towards a more positive evaluation of marriage and sexuality. The English *Book of Common Prayer* is notable, for instance, in including among the purposes of marriage 'the mutual society, help, and comfort, that the one ought to have of the other, both in prosperity and adversity'. Though it stands alongside starkly Augustinian strictures on the darker aspects of sexuality, here is the welcome beginning of some account of sexual love in the Church's theology of marriage.

All Christian traditions have built enthusiastically upon this in the ensuing centuries, reflecting and encouraging wider cultural trends. The Enlightened critique of the doctrine of original sin (discussed in the chapter on reconciliation) brought with it a more positive evaluation of sexual desire. It was to be celebrated as truly human, not feared as squalid degradation. Marriage was not about disciplining brute instinct, but celebrating noble love. Greater emphasis was progressively placed on the quality of relationship between the bride and groom, until by the twentieth century this was considered by most westerners to be of paramount importance. Even if this ideal was often honoured in the breach, the rise of feminism in the twentieth century made this shift all but irreversible. Women refused to be defined as mere property good for breeding, and both sexes would now insist on mutually enriching love as the *sine qua non* of marriage. It seems we are back, at last, with the joy of Cana. So what might the theology of marriage look like today?

A joyful vision

When marriage was first defined as a sacrament it was on the grim grounds that only thus could sexual desire be saved from lust, and reproduction be sanctified. The Reformers denied it was a sacrament, on the grounds that only baptism and eucharist had been commanded by Jesus. Does it matter whether we think of marriage as a sacrament, and is there a more joyful way to do so than the medievals offered? The answer to both questions is an emphatic 'yes'.

Sacraments happen when Jesus lays hold of a human action, and makes it the form of his own. Through what people do with each other, Jesus acts in his characteristic way, as in Galilee and on the cross: leaping out of himself in love, healing relationships, making people bearers of his joy. Sacraments both signify what is happening, and make it happen. Jesus acts to make those who perform the outward and visible sign truly participate in the inward and spiritual reality: the joy of his risen life.

In marriage, the outward and visible sign is the loving relationship between a man and woman (the possibility of same-sex marriage will be discussed shortly). To say that marriage is a sacrament is to say that the joy of Jesus becomes incarnate in that relationship. It is not just that Jesus approves of marriages. Rather, the love which a man and woman have for each other becomes a way in which they – and wider society – are caught up in joy happening, in the risen life of Jesus surging through human relationships to make them like him: utterly loving, utterly joyful. As with bread and wine in the eucharist, there is no competition between the created reality and the grace which it bears. The bread, as bread, feeds us with Jesus. The sexual love, as itself, does the same. Grace does not abolish nature, but perfects it.

This returns us to Paul's very bad argument in 1 Corinthians 7.32–35 that marriage necessarily involves second-rate discipleship, as spouses' devotion will be divided between Jesus and their lover. That only holds if their mutual love is considered as something essentially alien from, and therefore in potential competition with, their relationship with Jesus. If marriage is a sacrament, however, then Jesus lays hold of the marital relationship and makes himself the deepest truth of it. When a husband loves his wife, he is loving Jesus – and if the homoerotic overtones disturb, remember that after Easter and Pentecost 'Jesus' now means not an isolated male figure but the great spring of joy welling up to embrace all humanity. There simply is no competition between Jesus and the beloved: which is why the *Book of Common Prayer* wedding vows can include the startling words, 'With my body, I thee *worship* . . .' On Paul's logic in 1 Corinthians 7, that is idolatry. If marriage is a sacrament, it makes perfect sense.

Of course, the relationship to the spouse might come into conflict with the relationship to Jesus. It will do so, however, only insofar as it fails to be truly itself – a genuinely joyful, loving relationship. If one partner manipulates and exploits the other, the marriage is not as it should be and there is a tension between the sacramental sign and the joy of Jesus. If the couple shut themselves up in selfish defensiveness against the world, the sign fails. It is cases like these which could justify Paul's anxieties, or indeed Jesus' disturbing challenges to family obligations. However, they happen only when marriages fail to be what they are meant to be: outward and visible signs of the joy of Jesus, signs which make that joy happen for the partners and the world around.

Marriages fail all the time, and not just when they end in divorce. They fail like ordinations or even baptisms fail – because human beings are lifted by these acts into a reality for which we are not yet ready, into perfect joy. We fail to live out our truth all the time, to greater or lesser degrees. And this underlines the importance of marriage being a sacrament. Sacraments represent Jesus' promise to go on sharing his joy, with utter fidelity, in and through all our inadequacies. We need to know that joy is there, even when it seems absent. And crucially, we need to know that it has laid hold of us and longs to bring our faltering attempts at loving to perfection. The medieval Church was right that sacramental grace saves marriage from sinfulness. Its mistake was to see that sin solely in terms of sexual desire and intercourse. We need marriage to be a sacrament because we are bad lovers in a much wider sense, and need joy to rush in to heal our poor loving.

If marriage is a perfect expression of joy, it must also be fruitful. Joy always wants to celebrate itself, to burst out of its own life and make there be other realities which can rejoice with it. The first chapter suggested that this is the ultimate reason for creation's very existence – because the joy which God is yearns for expression, to share itself. The most characteristic way in which human marriage reflects and joins in that joy is through procreation (a significant word, echoing the primal act of joy's fruitfulness). We cannot say that it is only when man and woman have a child that they fully reflect and share in the *imago dei*: Jesus himself was neither husband nor father. However, it is striking that Genesis 1 speaks of humanity being in the *imago dei* precisely in the context of sexual difference and reproduction. Having children in marriage may not be the only way in which humans are *imago dei*, but it does seem at least an obvious – even the normal – way in which they may be.

However, there is more to marriage's fruitfulness than procreation. The social significance of marriage has already been alluded to: a relationship of joy should be a source of joy to all around it. Like the ordained, the married are meant to be 'walking sacraments': the quality of their love for each other should strengthen and inspire loving relationships all around them, should be the way in which the joy of Jesus rushes in to heal and renew lives other than their own. Marriages bear fruit in countless different ways, long after procreation has passed from the agenda.

The most fundamental way in which they do so is by making outward and visible the inward and spiritual truth of all human community. Understandably, human beings don't trust each other very much. We have spent too much of history killing each other to hope that the deepest truth of all things is actually otherwise, that we might really be bound together in life-giving joy. Marriage says that we are. This was the vision glimpsed by the author of Ephesians, and given a central place in all contemporary marriage liturgies: that marriage reveals the mystery of Jesus' union with the Church and ultimately with the world. What is reality really like? Not in the end, marriage says, like people set against each other, consumed and consuming. Rather, because of Jesus, 'the world is a wedding':[85] lives coming together in joy, fruitfully. Marriage tells the world its true nature and destiny, and gives us courage to reach towards it.

Difficult questions

How might this joyful vision stand up against some of the difficult questions posed to the Christian understanding of marriage today? What, for instance, of the common perception that Christian teaching on marriage and sexuality is unrealistic? The Church holds that sexual intercourse belongs exclusively within marriage. Marital sex is good; all other sex is sinful. This view however is spectacularly disregarded not just by the general population but by many Christians. Of course, people dissemble about sexual practice, but nearly twenty years ago a major study of sexual behaviour in the UK concluded that less than 1 per cent of 16–24-year-olds who had experienced sexual intercourse were married when they first did so.[86] Today, at least 70 per cent of couples live together before they are married. Given such facts, should the Church insist that sexual intercourse before marriage is sinful?

---

85 The phrase belongs to A. M. Allchin, 1978, *The World is a Wedding: Explorations in Christian Spirituality*, London: Darton, Longman and Todd.

86 K. Wellings, J. Field, A. M. Johnson and J. Wadsworth, 1994, *Sexual Behaviour in Britain: The National Survey of Sexual Attitudes and Lifestyles*, Harmondsworth: Penguin, p. 72.

And what about same-sex marriage? At its heart, this is a question of the role of procreation and sexual difference in marriage. On most Christian accounts, both have a central role to play which would rule out the prospect of same-sex marriage. However, on closer inspection we will see that the case is not so sure. Quite possibly, opening the prospect of same-sex marriage is going to be the next big development in the theology of marriage (and as we have seen, that theology does indeed develop).

A third controversial question is that of divorce and remarriage. It is one thing to emphasize that because marriage is a sacrament, Jesus will go on giving himself to the partners through their mutual love despite all their sin and inadequacy. That sounds credible and important much of the time. What though when a couple have become poison to each other, when all that passes between them is bitterness and even violence? Can their marriage end, not only legally but spiritually? And if so, what happens to the partners – are they free to find love again, and make a marriage again?

First, the realism of Christian teaching on sex before marriage. The most important step in the argument, perhaps, is to make a crucial distinction we have neglected so far: a marriage is not the same thing as a wedding, and might exist long before one happens. That might sound a startling and unorthodox claim, but there is much warrant for it in Christian history. It was not until the eleventh century that a church liturgy came to be considered a normal element of marriage. Yet people had of course been viewed as married before then – because marriage was not seen as something which the Church or priest effected for a couple, but something that they did with each other. Their marriage existed in their complete sharing of life together. The Church witnessed this, but did not create it. This insight has been an enduring element in the western theology of marriage. Accordingly, long after the eleventh century, the *Book of Common Prayer* still carefully entitles the relevant liturgy as 'The Solemnization of Matrimony' – suggesting, one commentator notes, that 'matrimony, or the state of being married, has already been entered into. It has to have started in order to be solemnized.'[87]

In fact, until the late eighteenth century most couples in most of Western Europe lived and slept together before their wedding day. The upper echelons of society maintained (in public at least) a different morality, the virginity of rich women being much prized in the marriage market. But throughout the eighteenth century, half of all brides in Britain and North America were pregnant on their wedding day – and this was not a cause for scandal or surprise.[88] Such couples were following a centuries-old two-stage pattern of marriage. First came the state of betrothal, when lovers would make a serious but not irrevocable commitment to each other as prospective partners in marriage. This was a period of growing together – of living together, and sleeping together – settling into the relationship, seeing if the future would work, undertaken with every intention of making it work. It was, then, rather like what many couples do today.

It was assumed, of course, that when children came the couple would take the further step of public and irrevocable commitment: 'the solemnization of matrimony'. In an age before contraception, this meant that the period of betrothal was generally short. In our changed circumstances, the period of 'betrothal' is accordingly rather longer, sometimes of

---

87 Adrian Thatcher, 2003, *The Guide to Christian Marriage and to Getting Married in Church*, London: Continuum, p. 77.

88 L. Stone, 'Passionate Attachments in the West in Historical Perspective', in K. Scott and M. Warren, eds, 1993, *Perspectives on Marriage: A Reader*, Oxford: Oxford University Press, p. 176.

indefinite duration. This presents its own dilemmas: women, for instance, sometimes fear that men in such a situation will never take the final step of public, irrevocable commitment. Nevertheless, this history dispels the idea that traditional Christian teaching on sex holds that it has no place before the wedding day. It has no place, rather, outside of a relationship which is steadily and determinedly developing into marriage – but that is a rather subtler proposition.

Some Christians might fear that this revision of Christian teaching is simply an accommodation to prevailing cultural standards and an excuse for sexual permissiveness. Remember, however, the kind of revision it is: a return to traditional Christian teaching and practice. It is the period *c.*1800–*c.*1960, with its isolated focus upon the wedding as opposed to the marriage, which marks the real departure from tradition. More important than pedigree, though, is the fact that the practice recalled here both reflects how people actually live and grow, and represents a serious call to holiness.

Reflecting how people live and grow is not simply code for adapting to changed cultural norms and patterns of sinfulness. This is realism about intimacy and how it is, emotionally and physically, a developmental process. People grow into love and marriage over time: it does not happen in an instant. And as the inward and spiritual reality grows gradually, so does the outward and visible expression – sexual behaviour. The idea, often fostered in 'conservative' Christian circles, that couples should go from not much more than holding hands one day to full intercourse the next, simply does not match how human beings work. Those who teach it are asking to be ignored, and, on the rare occasions they are not, risk grave damage to those who follow their advice.

Moreover, the older and saner approach makes genuine moral demands. Obviously, it challenges the culture of promiscuity by teaching that full sexual expression belongs only within a relationship where both parties fully intend to share all of life together. That is stern enough, but it also places a great responsibility upon couples to honestly assess what their relationship means, and when different kinds of sexual expression might be right – true outward and visible signs of an inward and spiritual reality, which help that reality to happen. It calls for sexual wisdom rather than a rulebook, and wisdom is always the more challenging demand. That is especially so in matters sexual, where the temptation to delude and indulge oneself is potent. The temptation to rigidly regulate and codify sexual practice is eminently understandable – but it is a temptation, and should be resisted.

So why have a wedding at all? At one level, it is a very good question: marriage is what matters, and marriages exist without weddings. Arguably, though, it is like the Church and bishops. The Church would exist without bishops, but bishops are still a very good idea. So are weddings, for at least two reasons.

First, there is something strange about a couple who claim to fully share their lives together with total commitment and yet are unwilling to publicly say so. The public recognition of marriage – which is what a wedding does – is sometimes derided as a mere 'piece of paper', but R. C. Moberly's point is seldom more obviously true than here: 'spirit corresponds with body, as body with spirit; and those who have tried to cut loose from what seemed to them merely outward, find more and more, in fact, that in losing reality of body they have been losing reality of spirit too'.[89] We know this is true. Research

89 R. C. Moberly, 1899, *Ministerial Priesthood: Chapters (Preliminary to a Study of the Ordinal) On the Rationale and the Meaning of Christian Priesthood, with an Appendix upon Roman Catholic Criticism of Anglican Orders*, London: John Murray, p. 55.

consistently shows that those who live together without ever becoming 'officially' married are significantly more likely to break up than those who do. It also consistently shows better life outcomes for children born to couples who are not merely cohabiting, but formally married.[90]

And that is the second reason for weddings: marriages are not just about the couple involved. The married are to be 'walking sacraments': they are to strengthen and inspire all around them to love. That holds not only for their children, but for their neighbours. A wonderful way to do this is to have a public celebration of marriage, where the couple proclaim what has happened between them and the community recognizes it. The community benefits, and the couple benefit: being a walking sacrament is hard, and they will need the love and support of all around them. If, as suggested above, marriage is rather like ordination, it is worth reflecting that an essential part of ordination is that candidates are recognized by, and prayed for by, their community. (It is also worth observing that the Church generally gives far more attention to discerning the vocation to ordination, and forming candidates, and supporting them through the years than it does in the case of marriage.)

One final thought about weddings. In the Roman Catholic and Orthodox tradition, the norm is to celebrate such occasions with the eucharist – a nuptial mass. In Reformed churches, this is relatively rare (although notably, the *Book of Common Prayer* exhorts the couple to receive communion together soon after the wedding). While there can be good pastoral reasons for this, it is a loss. The eucharist is the best

90 Recent evidence is well summarised in The Centre for Social Justice, 2010, *Green Paper on the Family*, Centre for Social Justice, Westminster. This is available online at www.centreforsocialjustice.org.uk.

possible way to understand what is happening in marriage, and the greatest assistance to those believers trying to live one. The heart of the eucharist is Jesus saying, 'this is my body, given for you . . .' As he says it, he gives his disciples the power to do it: to give their bodies for each other. And that is what bride and groom are called to do. They are to give themselves to each other, utterly, forever and without reserve, to make each other alive with joy – and through the eucharist Jesus will help them to do so. If there are pastoral reasons for separating the two sacraments, there are still weightier ones for putting them back together.

From weddings to the question of same-sex marriage. We must leave on one side here the hotly contested issue of what precisely the Scriptures teach about homosexual practice.[91] In a book about sacraments the question is rather: if homosexual relationships are not, by definition, sinful (at least, no more so than heterosexual ones – presumably there is some element of sinfulness in all relationships) then could a loving, monogamous, life-long homosexual partnership be a marriage?

At first sight, the question appears to boil down to what we think is the place of procreation within the purposes of marriage. On most Christian accounts, procreation is a prime purpose – if not the prime purpose – of marriage. A love which by definition cannot create new life could not therefore count as marriage, even if in many other ways splendid and virtuous.

---

91 Although cards should go on the table: Scripture does not address the question of loving monogamous same-sex relationships, except insofar as Jesus teaches the general ethical principle: 'By their fruits shall you know them.' Their fairly obvious good fruits suggest that such relationships cannot be, *ipso facto*, sinful.

However, this is a rather difficult stance to defend. It is no longer clear, for example, that the Church of England regards the intention to procreate as essential to marriage. References to procreation in the *Common Worship* marriage liturgy are tellingly optional. That is because the Church of England, far from uniquely, wants the freedom to conduct marriages where the woman may have already gone through the menopause, or where there are other medical reasons why a couple cannot have children. Nor does it want to shut the door on those couples who are quite open about their lack of intention to procreate for other personal reasons. There will be a range of pastoral responses in such cases, but few would say that the right response would always be to refuse to marry the couple. Yet that would be the logical corollary of making either the intention or capability to reproduce essential to marriage.

If not procreation, then perhaps sexual difference remains essential: might there be something important about the fact that marriage is male and female coming together, which would be missing in a same-sex union? This is not a stupid idea. It has deep echoes in Scripture, and many people instinctively feel there is something to it. However, it is remarkably difficult to get any further than instinct. It suggests some perceived spiritual difference between men and women which is expressed through physical difference, but lies beyond it (an inward and spiritual reality, given outward and visible form . . .). Yet every attempt to articulate that difference ends in embarrassment: in saying, for instance, that women are somehow essentially 'receptive' and men essentially 'active', or that women are naturally submissive and men naturally authoritative (shades of debates about ordination here). All such attempts die amidst hilarity, outrage or a thousand qualifications. So even though the instinct that tradition is not stupid remains strong, it does not afford a well-worked-out rationale for refusing same sex marriage.

And the case *for* such marriage seems persuasive. Homosexual Christians seem to experience the love they share with each other as the form of Jesus' love for them, as heterosexual couples do. Their love seems to be fruitful, in their own lives and the lives of others around them, as heterosexual marriage is (not least, frequently, in the care of children). In short, joy seems to be happening here: something 'holy' is happening. Theirs is rather more than a purely legal arrangement, as the term 'civil partnership' seems to suggest. It is a journey into joy, which looks remarkably like marriage. The instinctive importance given to sexual difference should certainly give the Church pause for thought before it declares same-sex unions to be marriages. But that thought might well in the end reach a positive conclusion. And if it does, it is worth remembering that we are really dealing with quite a small number of people here. It is hard to imagine, despite all the shrill warnings, that heterosexual marriage will somehow be done grave harm by letting a few people of the same sex marry. They might even show heterosexuals how it is done: that's what walking sacraments do.

It is striking how many opponents of same-sex marriage have reconciled themselves with remarkable ease to the practice of divorce and remarriage. This acceptance represents at least a comparable degree of change in the institution and theology of marriage. Admittedly, Roman Catholicism has never accepted remarriage after divorce, while the Orthodox have always allowed it in certain circumstances – the teaching of both churches remaining therefore quite unchanged. For others, though, the change has been dramatic. In 1936, the Supreme Governor of the Church of England was forced to abdicate because he wished to marry a divorcee. Today the next Supreme Governor has already married a divorcee, and had this marriage liturgically blessed.[92] The number of church weddings involving one or more divorcees is rising year on year in the Church of England and many other Reformed churches. It is increasingly considered rather unusual and unattractively strict for clergy in these churches to refuse to preside over such services.

This is truly remarkable. Jesus was very clear: 'So they are no longer two, but one flesh. Therefore what God has joined together, let no one separate . . . Whoever divorces his wife and marries another commits adultery against her; and if she divorces her husband and marries another, she commits adultery' (Mark 10.8–12). Divorce then seems not only wrong, but in a sense *impossible*: you might leave your spouse, even obtain a legal divorce, but at the most real level of all you would still be married. If these words are taken at face value, marriages are quite simply indissoluble. As C. S. Lewis once wrote in a related context: 'the truth is that wherever a man lies with a woman, there, whether they like it or not, a transcendental relation is set up between them which must be eternally enjoyed or

92 Some might protest that in Charles' case, it was not the Marriage Service which was used but the 'The Order for Prayer and Dedication after a Civil Marriage'. However, the latter service casts no doubt on the fact that what is being celebrated is a true marriage, and includes provision for blessing the couple. There is no real theological distinction between it and the Marriage Service. The only real effect of requiring divorcees to use the different service is to convey a certain reserve or disapproval concerning their new marriages – which is then contradicted by blessing them! The practice is theologically incoherent and pastorally crass.

eternally endured'.[93] (A problem lurks in these words to which we will return.)

How then can Christians justify remarriage after divorce? The question is actually whether Christians can believe in divorce as a spiritual reality and not merely a legal fiction: whether marriages can truly die, spiritually speaking. If so, then it follows the parties are no longer married, and equally that there is no reason why they cannot marry again. There might be sensible pastoral grounds for suggesting to individuals that to do so would be unwise. But those individuals would now be unmarried, and hence in principle free to marry again.

The Roman Catholic Church, like many Christians beyond it, thinks that Christians are not free to follow this reasoning. Rome acknowledges divorce as a reality in civil law, but believes that those who have undergone this process nonetheless remain married in God's eyes. Hence they cannot marry again, and those who do (in civil ceremonies) are officially barred from receiving the eucharist unless they commit to living in chastity. It is a controversial and hard policy, with the usual Roman merits of tough-minded consistency and refusal to accommodate to prevailing cultural mores. Christians who disagree must be very careful lest they end in collaborating with sin. Divorce damages people, especially children, and is resorted to far too often and far too quickly in our culture. The Church must be deeply wary of doing anything which seems to normalize it or trivialize its cost.

All that said, there remain good reasons for thinking that divorce and remarriage might be a legitimate Christian option. First, remember the particular context into which Jesus' stern prohibition was uttered. He was addressing a culture

93 C. S. Lewis, 1942, *The Screwtape Letters*, London: Collins, p. 94.

where not only was divorce easy, but its effect was devastating. According to some schools of Jewish law, men could divorce women in first-century Israel pretty much at whim: lightly, casually. And when they did, those women were left destitute and pathetically vulnerable. When Jesus outlawed divorce, what he was doing was saying to men: 'You can't treat women like rubbish.' And so his prohibition on divorce belongs naturally within his ministry of joy – the inauguration of a Kingdom where no one would be treated like rubbish.

What then would he have said here, now? It is at least plausible that he would have opposed divorces where people are treated like rubbish, and marriages where people are treated like rubbish. It is at least plausible that he would acknowledge that sometimes it is precisely divorce which allows people to stand up straight and claim their dignity. Some marriages crush people, and arguably what joy would do is set them free. So it is not obvious that in being true to the letter of Jesus' saying we are true to the spirit in which he said it.

That might sound like tendentious evasion of the plain sense of Jesus' words. However, that 'plain sense' is in need of careful examination. *Contra* Mark, there is some ambiguity about Jesus' teaching. In Matthew 5.32 and 19.9, he allows that adultery might end a marriage, and that the innocent party in such a situation is free to marry again. Yet marriages are either indissoluble, or they are not. If they can be dissolved after adultery, why not after desertion or violence? Or simply when the marriage has decayed from a life-giving love into stifling resentment and hostility? The 'Matthean exception' might open the door to something like contemporary Reformed and historic Orthodox practice.

A slippery slope beckons. Who will judge which situations might be covered by the Matthean exception, and which not? We could end with divorce being justified on all sorts of dubious grounds. Would it not be wiser to stick to what the text actually says: that adultery alone provides the basis for ending a marriage? Such an approach would have the additional advantage of taking seriously one of the insights of the traditional theology of marriage: sexual intercourse really matters. This instinct was present in the medieval idea that marriage makes sex less sinful, and sanctifies human reproduction. It flowers in the much richer contemporary theology of marriage, which sees intercourse as, par excellence, an outward and visible sign of the inward and spiritual grace of marriage: the fleshly coming together of lives in fruitful joy. In either perspective, intercourse is at the heart of marriage. Adulterous intercourse, therefore, could be seen as striking at that heart, an especially grievous assault capable of killing the marriage. So would run a 'conservative' argument aimed at restricting the grounds of divorce to adultery. The argument for absolute indissolubility, remember, is already lost in the Matthean exception.

However, if we must hold fast to what the Matthean exception allows without extending it further, note that what Matthew allows is for the husband to divorce his wife. The provision does not run both ways. This little-noticed fact often causes great surprise when pointed out to contemporary readers. However, until quite recent times it was not considered unusual. In cultures where wives were regarded primarily as property and as material for breeding, an adulterous married woman not only sinned against her lord's property rights but risked inveigling another man's child into his inheritance. Male adultery by contrast (as long as it was not with a married woman) had no such consequences and therefore was judged not so catastrophically sinful. This was a perfectly usual interpretation of the Matthean exception until at least the eighteenth century.[94] We may be appalled, and rightly claim liberty to reinterpret what Jesus said in the light of his broader teaching and principles – but if we do, we are going beyond the actual scope of the Matthean exception and the slippery slope looms again.

Second, while there is undoubtedly something powerful and true in seeing sexual intercourse as near the heart of marriage, we can also take sex *too* seriously. Richard Holloway has wisely observed, 'history has burdened the Christian experience of sex with unusual tensions, loading a natural reality with too much supernatural consequence'.[95] Take the words of C. S. Lewis, quoted above, about the transcendental bond set up 'whenever a man lies with a woman', to be eternally enjoyed or endured. That is a very strong view of the sacramentality of sex, pushing it to the point where intercourse becomes the constitutive sign of marriage, the deed which creates marriage. It reads wonderfully, and leads to bizarre and terrible conclusions. Granted that most people have more than one sexual partner in their lifetimes, most marriages are in fact adulterous or polygamous unions. Worse still, a woman is married to her rapist: the bond is set up between them 'whether they like it or not'.

Such conclusions follow from focusing exclusively on the act of intercourse as opposed to the wider relationship in which it occurs. We know they are ridiculous, and that it is the wider relationship to which we must pay attention. As

94 See for example the 1644 view of the influential English theologian Henry Hammond, cited in P. E. More and F. L. Cross, eds, 1935, *The Thought and Practice of the Church of England*, London: SPCK, pp. 662–3.

95 Richard Holloway, 1997, *Dancing on the Edge*, London: Fount, p. 98.

soon as we do that, however, making adulterous intercourse the *one* thing which can undo the marital bond loses all plausibility. Which is the bigger betrayal: the adulterous 'one-night stand' or the emotional desertion of spouse for career, or the sustained reign of domestic violence? Reason compels a wider interpretation of the Matthean exception and opens the way to allowing divorce and remarriage.

One further obstacle remains. Marriage is meant to represent the union of Christ with his Church, the way in which joy weds itself irrevocably to human lives. This book has repeatedly rhapsodized about the fidelity which is signified and enabled through sacraments, about how Jesus goes on giving himself to and through his people regardless of the poverty of their response to him. In baptism, Jesus makes himself the deepest reality of a person's life in a way that can never be undone, even if that person never responds to the joy beating within. In reconciliation, the penitent is absolved even if their response to that absolution is pathetically inadequate. In ordination, Jesus promises to act through the ordained even if they are mired in deep and unrepented sin. The promises Jesus makes in the sacraments – his marriage vows to his people – are unbreakable. So mustn't the sacrament of marriage be unbreakable too?

This is the theological heart of the indissolubilist tradition. It undoubtedly has great spiritual appeal. It feels right, it makes the deep kind of aesthetic moral sense which rings true within the Christian conscience and imagination. And indeed, marriage is meant to be forever. Divorce, however necessary it might be, always means a spiritual catastrophe has happened. The death of a marriage grievously wounds the couple, their children and the community for whom they were walking sacraments.

Yet we must not confuse what should be the case with what is. Sometimes, marriages die. People can become the bearers of hate to each other, rather than love. Strict indissolubilists say that, nevertheless, the marital bond endures. They do so from the best of motives, but with terrible consequences. To say that those who find themselves in this desolate state must spend the rest of their lives without sexual intimacy is to impose a burden which few can bear. In the name of preserving inviolate a sacramental sign long devoid of actual life, men and women are required to renounce the call to sexual intimacy which Scripture and experience suggest is deeply inscribed within most hearts: 'it is not good that the man should be alone' (Genesis 2.18). It is no coincidence that the denomination, which takes the hardest line on this is also that whose doctrine and discipline, is most determined by celibates. Their forebears despised sex and marriage; now they idealize it to such an extent that its failure cannot be accepted. Nor can they quite understand why, when it does fail, the men and women involved cannot embrace the celibate life. The abiding error is a failure of realism.

And that error is not just pastoral, but theological: one of the most seductive for those who love the sacraments. It is the temptation of confusing signs with the thing signified. Yes, Christ's union with the Church, joy's union with the world, is indissoluble. Even the gates of hell shall not prevail against it. Yes, that union is signified in and lives through human marriage; just like joy is signified in, and lives through the Church. Yet in neither case are outward sign and inward reality point blank identical. Grace does not abolish nature. Bread remains bread. There is a sense in which Jesus lives in the Church and the sacraments, emphasized throughout this book. Yet, nearing the end we must sound the crucial counterpoint: there is also a sense in which he does *not*. There was a glory greater than marriage at Cana. The Church and the sacraments remain *signs*: realities which point to a joy far beyond themselves. 'Now we see but in a glass darkly; then we shall see face to face' (1 Corinthians 13.12). And so, to the final chapter.

FOR DISCUSSION

- Where do you see the lasting effects of Christianity's historic anxiety about sexuality? Are there any in your church?
- What would be the wisest teaching about sex and marriage to give to teenagers?
- How should the Church prepare people for marriage, and support them once they are married?
- What circumstances would make it right for the Church to refuse to celebrate a marriage?
- Why have many churches found it easier to accept remarriage after divorce than same-sex marriage?

FOR REFLECTION

In our living together we are one another's hands, ears and feet. Marriage redoubles our strength, rejoices our friends, causes grief to our enemies. A common concern makes trials bearable. Common joys are all the happier, and accord makes riches more pleasant; it is even more delightful than riches for those without wealth. Marriage is the key of moderation and the harmony of the desires, the seal of a deep friendship . . . United in the flesh, one in spirit, they urge each other on by the goad of their mutual love. For marriage does not remove from God,

but brings all the closer to him, for it is God himself who draws us to it.
Gregory of Nazianzus[96]

And so I praise marriage because it brings forth virgins. Thus do I gather the rose from the thorns, the gold from the earth, the pearl from the shell.
Jerome[97]

God's word is actually inscribed on one's spouse. When a man looks at his wife as if she were the only woman on earth, and when a woman looks at her husband as if he were the only man on earth; yes, if no king or queen, not even the sun itself sparkles any more brightly and lights up your eyes more than your own husband or wife, then right there you are face to face with God speaking. God promises to you your wife or husband, actually gives your spouse to you saying, 'The man shall be yours. I am pleased beyond measure! Creatures earthly and heavenly are jumping for joy.' For there is no jewellery more precious than God's Word; through it you come to regard your spouse as a gift of God and, as long as you do that, you have no regrets.
Marin Luther[98]

Only if I give myself entirely, without keeping any part of me back or being involved just until further notice, until, so

96 Gregory of Nazianzus, *In Praise of Virginity*, pp. 223–77.
97 Jerome, *Letter 22 to Eustachia.*
98 The reference is from a 1531 wedding sermon, included in the Weimarar Ausgabe collection of Luther's works, *WA* 24:52:12–21.

to speak, I find something better, does this fully correspond to human dignity. Human life is not an experiment. This is not a commercial contract, but a surrender of myself to another person. Only in the form of a love that is entire and unreserved is the self-giving of one person to another commensurate with the essence of man.
Benedict XVI[99]

United Christian families are a sign that love, unity and peace are possible. These families are, each in their own way, the first cell of all unity, of all forgiveness, of all community, of all fecundity. They are thus signs of hope.
Jean Vanier[100]

99 Joseph Ratzinger, 2002, *God and the World: A Conversation with Peter Seewald*, San Francisco: Ignatius, pp. 426–7.
100 Jean Vanier, 1985, *Man and Woman He Made Them*, London: Darton, Longman and Todd, p. 129.

8

The end of sacraments

What is the end of the sacraments? The question has two senses: what do they point towards? And what is their real importance? A good way to approach an answer is to think just a little more about marriage.

The preparation for a wedding can be difficult. Couples very often have their own priorities and ideas for the service which do not always coincide with those of the Church or officiating minister and a fraught set of negotiations can ensue. 'Bride-zilla' is a well-known monster to the clergy. However, in many traditions the one part of the service which floats serenely above all such discussions is the wedding vows. Not only do most people think the set form of words does the job admirably, but in the Church of England at any rate to deviate from the set form is to risk rendering the marriage illegal – mention of this usually has the desired effect of stifling enthusiastic creativity on the part of those wishing to be wed.

So I was surprised when one day a thoughtful couple, both committed Christians and not displaying any 'Bride-zilla' tendencies, told me that they had a serious objection to the wording of the vows and wished not to use them. My initial, puzzled, concern that they might somehow be seeking to qualify or minimize the radical self-gift involved in the vows was however misplaced. Their problem was with the words, '. . . until death do us part'. As far as they were concerned, death would not mark the end of their marriage. They would be together, forever.

A dry pastoral response would have been to ask what each would do if, God forbid, the other was to die much more quickly than expected. Yet the question they raised was not a silly one. They echoed the sentiment which is so strong in many people's hearts and minds: that love must be stronger than death, that in some sense our loved ones can never be torn from us. Christians cannot call that mere sentiment. If man and woman are made one flesh by marriage, and if we believe in the resurrection of the body, then surely people will be raised as they have lived: fused together for all eternity?

That seems logical, but goes against the direct teaching of Jesus. The Sadduccees, who did not believe in the resurrection, once tried to show its foolishness by asking this kind of question. Once there was an exceptionally unlucky woman who married, in turn, no less than seven brothers – making her way through the family as each one of them died. In the resurrection, then, whose wife will she be? My prospective marriage couple might be stumped by such a question. Jesus' reply, however, was emphatic: 'You are wrong, because you know neither the Scriptures nor the power of God. For in the resurrection they neither marry nor are given in marriage, but are like angels in heaven' (Matthew 22.23–33; Mark 12.18–27; Luke 20.27–40). Luke's version speaks in terms of 'ages': marriage is for the people of this age. In the age to come, it has no place.

This returns us to the basic instinct described as the heart of marriage at the very beginning of the last chapter. To be married is to embrace 'the human thing': to give a vote of confidence in the future and testify to the deep-down desire in each of us that our lives belong to some bigger story, that life is not just a matter of our own private existence which will decline and disappear. The most instinctive way to state this faith is to have children. We each die, but the bigger 'we' goes on. The race will strive and never surrender. At the most fundamental biological and spiritual level, the reason for marriage and procreation is to raise a great protest against death.

However, the gospel is that one day death will be no more. There will be nothing left to protest against. For Jesus Christ has been raised from the dead, and joy has already begun to ripple from his empty tomb through all creation, freeing people from death's power. We see that now as lives are set free and healed, as joy becomes the truth of relationships that were once locked in hostility and fear, as the truth dawns on people that there is nothing left to fear. The first chapter suggested that that was what experience of the resurrection means. Yet what dawns must sometime break into full daylight. Our present ambiguous, fragmentary experience of joy must one be day be swept up into the reality itself. The Kingdom will come.

In most mainstream churches, there is a remarkable coyness around this area of Christian doctrine, known as eschatology. That is in part due to the long history of idiocy with which it has been handled: the many failed predictions of the end of the world, and the over-detailed timetables for Jesus' second coming beloved of many. It is also due to a slow seepage of fundamental conviction: a loss of the sense that the story of the world is actually one story at all, let alone one aimed at a glorious destiny. Accordingly, if eschatology gets handled at all by many churches, it tends to be reduced to speculation about the 'after-life' of individuals or ethical exhortations to work together now to build the Kingdom of God on earth.

This represents a catastrophic loss in Christianity. The gospel is that the joy of Jesus will become the deepest truth of all creation, healing it definitively and allowing all who will – and in the end, we dare hope that means *all* – to become nothing but joy. It is simply impossible to articulate that gospel without something like a comprehensive eschatological vision, without belief in the realities that traditionally have been indicated by phrases like 'the end of the world' or 'he will come again in glory, to judge the living and the dead'. It might take another book to fully defend the claim, but if Christianity gives up this hope it has given up the gospel and should itself be given up.

We are of course incapable of giving much precise content to the glory which awaits, of describing what the utter triumph of joy shall look like when it happens. That is the error of the overconfident apocalyptic fringe which so embarrasses mainstream Christianity. Yet it is an even greater error to suppose that because we cannot describe something adequately, it is not real or not going to happen. The entire point is that the joyous glory which awaits us is *so* joyous and *so* glorious that it outstrips our resources not only to produce, but even to imagine. We are incapable of it; it will come as sheer gift. Meanwhile, all we can do is trace the glimmers of the great dawn already piercing through the night. We eagerly look for and celebrate the moments when we can see and are seized by the powers of the age to come, already surging towards us and within us. And one of the principal ways we do so is by celebrating sacraments.

So take marriage. In it the end is glimpsed, because human lives are lived as they are meant to be and will be;

as a joyous, fruitful coming together. Individuals are no longer held apart from each other, in hostility or loneliness. Rather, they are fused together, not so as to lose their individuality but to receive it anew, perfected through the love of their partner. People are made gifts to each other, made the way in which the joy of Jesus wells up to engulf each other in transfiguring power. Together, they become an ecstasy of joy: the *imago dei*. Now, we live in history and are sinners. Marriage will not always feel like an ecstasy of joy. But that is what is trying to break through history and sinfulness, and what lovers are caught up in. We glimpse it now just in couples, and poorly even in them. We will know it one day as the deepest truth of all things.

Which means, returning to the young couple with which this chapter began, that there is a sense in which they will be married for eternity *and* a sense in which they will not. For their marriage reveals the deepest truth not only of their lives, but of all things. In this age, as limited beings we glimpse truth in limited ways – in marriage to one other person, and then with difficulty. In the age to come, we shall be love without limit. *All* lives (we hope) will be fused together, made gifts to each other, made perfectly themselves through each other, engulfed together in transfiguring joy (a full investigation of Paul's theology of the resurrection of the body would bring us to the same conviction). As a tipsy theologian once put it, 'Heaven means sex with everyone.' He was profoundly correct. What sex between lovers means at its best now is the stuff of our life to come. This is why so many religions have featured cultic orgies or temple prostitution: it is not just an excuse for lust (though it may be that too!), but a reflection of the profound connection sensed between sexuality and the call which summons all flesh to glory. Christianity expresses this in marriage. But when what marriages point to happens, they themselves shall fall away. There will only be the new reality: eternal joy.

So it is with all sacraments. In every chapter, the end of each sacrament has been seen to be eternal joy. Baptism and confirmation are the ways in which joy lays hold of a person, and claims their lives for its own. The baptized and the confirmed are knitted into the surging joy of Jesus, publicly joined to the community which knows the deepest truth of its life to be transfiguring grace. The marks of sin remain, but baptism means people are no longer defined by sin. They are publicly claimed, surrounded and acted on by joy. What has been done for them by Jesus may take beyond a lifetime to awaken response in them, but nevertheless baptism has set them towards their destiny, towards eternal joy.

The eucharist is the great feast of sharing. In it, human relationships and material goods – bread and wine – are signified as, and made, the stuff of joy. Lives and treasures which were hoarded against each other are caught up in the power of 'this is my body, given for you'. The sacrifice of Jesus, sharing, becomes the deepest energy running through human lives. His sharing is known to be so capable, so infinitely resourceful that in this feast even the division between living and dead is called into question. At eucharists now we know all this in theory and experience glimmers of its power, but as most liturgies testify in some form the eschatological surge is always there: 'As we eat this bread and drink this cup, we proclaim your death, Lord Jesus, *until you come in glory*.' Humanity is destined for a still greater feast, with angels and archangels and the whole company of heaven.

Ordination makes people visible bonds of this great company of saints extended across space and time. It is one of the ways in which we know that the twenty-first-century English church belongs to the same family as the seventeenth-century Chinese or fourth-century Greek one. Jesus also lays hold of these people to promise that, through them, he will always be pouring his joy into the Church to sustain and renew it. Yet, when the end comes there will be no need to symbolize belonging together because the reality will be inconceivably more evident than even lovemaking or feasting are now. There will be no need for ministers of sacraments, or preachers: 'No longer shall they teach one another, or say to each other, "Know the LORD", for they shall all know me, from the least of them to the greatest, says the LORD' (Jeremiah 31.34). St John the Divine puts it even better: 'I saw no temple in the city, for its temple is the Lord God the Almighty and the Lamb. And the city has no need of sun or moon to shine on it, for the glory of God is its light, and its lamp is the Lamb' (Revelation 21.22–23). No temple, no priests – just joy.

In reconciliation, Jesus deals with everything which would choke this. Sin is when I do something that obstructs joy, which stops me giving and receiving it as best I can – and hence it is never a purely private matter. Sin may be secret, but that in itself means I am not wholly made a gift to all others. Something of me is held back. In the sacrament of reconciliation, the penitent does their best to undo that, to expose their whole being before another Christian for love and healing. Properly undertaken, it is a magnificent experience. Yet no one's self-knowledge and penitence is ever perfect, and however great the confessor she is only one person. So the sacrament is but a glimmer of the glory: when we will have no secrets hidden from anyone, and when that will not bring shame and humiliation but joy. Think of the things we have done to each other and that seems simply inconceivable – but that is why it is called the gospel.

Anointing is the moment when joy confronts death in the most obvious sense: as we sicken, and as this life draws to a close. Of all the sacraments, it is perhaps the one where the eschatological reference is most obvious. The dying are anointed not to reverse their dying, but to redescribe it: to let them face it as but the end of one way of being human – the finite, historical, fragile way. What happened in Jesus' death means that to come to the end of that way is simply to come nearer to what baptism meant – to total immersion in joy. To be anointed is to stand on the very edge of glory, and to be given the courage to enter in. All the sacraments have urged us to this place – but now it is time to leave them behind. Now it is time to see, face to face. What is left to say but Hallelujah?

******

Well, one more thing. The chapter on baptism raised a question which it ducked answering, and which is relevant to all the sacraments. If God is bringing the whole world to joy, then in what sense are sacraments necessary? Does it really matter whether someone is baptized, or celebrates the eucharist? Traditional theology has described these two sacraments as 'necessary for salvation'. Yet this book has suggested that salvation is rushing to embrace the whole world, with all-but-irresistible force. So what becomes of the traditional claim? Taking baptism to stand for both: if we are saved without baptism, why be baptized?

There simply is no salvaging the traditional claim if that involves casting doubt on the will and capacity of joy to reconcile all things, or rendering the destiny of the unbaptized perilously uncertain. A theology which cheerfully countenances God abandoning billions of his creatures to misery is utterly unworthy of Jesus. The fact that such theology has long haunted the Church (though, by grace, never uncontestedly so) is a good reason to give thanks that being Christian is not about simply repeating what Christians have said before. Theology must always be tested and reformed by the gospel. Damning the unbaptized is an ancient (indeed scriptural) teaching which we do well to lose.

The affirmation of the necessity of baptism for salvation did however have a point – and still does. Something can be necessary for the salvation of the world without every person or most people in the world undergoing it. Rather, the world needs *some* to be baptized, *some* to celebrate the eucharist and the other sacraments. It needs them not only because these will be the people in whom joy is beginning to happen – for the Spirit blows beyond the Church and makes joy beyond it too. But only where the gospel is proclaimed and the sacraments celebrated are there people who know what that joy means. Only in the Church does the world realize where it is going and what its true destiny is. Only gospel people can help the rest to see, and thus to know, true joy. The Church and the sacraments are necessary for salvation not in the sense that without them anyone is damned, but as brightening skies are 'necessary' before dawn. They are joy's ways of piercing through the night to touch us and strengthen us, to encourage and inspire – to help us live in the dark as people of light, confident that in just a little while day will break and the shadows flee.

Which means that rather a lot rides upon sacraments and the people who celebrate them. Both are to be signs of joy, the kinds of signs which not only point to the wonderful reality which awaits us all, but which begin to make it real here and now. For the sake of the world, the Church must be where human ruins are rebuilt, relationships are healed, sharing begins, and joy happens. We must be joy to the world. We will always be failing in that vocation, because we are as yet only the sign and not the thing signified. Yet in the end we shall not fail, because Jesus' promises – made in the sacraments – shall not fail. All our sin and misery cannot choke the joy of Jesus rising. He will always be there, always giving himself, surging in joy to meet and transfigure our poverty, and to finally carry us home. So now, what is left to say? 'Go therefore, and make disciples of all nations, baptizing them in the name of the Father and of the Son and of the Holy Spirit, and teaching them to obey everything that I have commanded you. And remember, I am with you always, to the end of the age' (Matthew 28.19–20).

FOR REFLECTION

> I consider that the sufferings of this present time are not worth comparing with the glory about to be revealed to us. For the creation waits with eager longing for the revealing of the children of God . . . the creation itself will be set free from its bondage to decay and will obtain the freedom of the glory of the children of God.
> *Romans 8.18–21*

> What we *usually* call 'Church' is that particular people which . . . announces, symbolizes, dramatizes the fact and possibility and promise of the common peoplehood, exceptionless communion, of the whole of humankind. The notorious slogan 'outside the church there is no

salvation' has always had two senses: that only Christians may be saved is false; that salvation is the healing of relations, the gathering of humankind into *ekklesia*, communion, in God, is true.
Nicholas Lash[101]

'Ah, but we want so much more . . . we do not want merely to *see* beauty though, God knows, even that is bounty enough. We want something else which can hardly be put into words – to be united with the beauty we see, to pass into it, to receive it into ourselves, to bathe in it, to become part of it . . . at the present we are on the outside of the world, the wrong side of the door. We discern the freshness and purity of morning, but they do not make us fresh and pure. We cannot mingle with the splendours we see. But all the leaves of the New Testament are rustling with the promise that it will not always be so. Some day, God willing, we shall get *in*.'
C. S. Lewis[102]

101 Nicholas Lash, 2004, *Holiness, Silence and Speech: Reflections on the Question of God*, Aldershot: Ashgate, p. 27.
102 C. S. Lewis, 1965, 'The Weight of Glory', in *Screwtape Proposes a Toast and Other Pieces*, London: Collins, p. 107.

Further reading

There is a huge amount of material available on the sacraments, and the following suggestions are not intended to be in any way exhaustive. However, each title recommended would provide a lively and accessible route into further discussion of sacramental theology and each particular sacrament.

An overview of the sacraments

Joseph Martos, 2001, *Doors to the Sacred: An Historical Introduction to Sacraments in the Catholic Church*, Collegeville: Liturgical Press.

Ross Thompson, 2006, *The SCM Studyguide to the Sacraments*, London: SCM Press.

Baptism and confirmation

Everett Fergusson, 2009, *Baptism in the Early Church: History, Theology and Liturgy in the First Five Centuries*, Grand Rapids: Eerdmans.

Aidan Kavanagh, 1988, *Confirmation: Origins and Reform*, New York: Peublo.

Thomas J. Nettles, Richard L. Pratt Jr, Robert Kolb and John D. Castelein, 2007, *Understanding Four Views on Baptism*, Grand Rapids: Zondervan.

Eucharist

Alasdair Heron, 1983, *Table and Tradition: Towards an Ecumenical Understanding of the Eucharist*, Edinburgh: Handsel Press.

Russell D. Moore, John I. Hesselink, David P. Scaer and Thomas A. Baima, 2007, *Understanding Four Views on the Lord's Supper*, Grand Rapids: Zondervan.

Kenneth Stevenson, 2002, *Do This: The Shape, Style and Meaning of the Eucharist*, Norwich: Canterbury Press.

Reconciliation

Martin Dudley and Geoffrey Rowell, eds, 1990, *Confession and Absolution*, London: SPCK.

John Stott, 1964, *Confess your Sins: The Way of Reconciliation*, London: Hodder and Stoughton.

Max Thurian, 1958, *Confession*, SCM Press, London.

Anointing

Martin Dudley and Geoffrey Rowell, eds, 1993, *The Oil of Gladness: Anointing in the Christian Tradition*, SPCK: London.

Martin Israel, 1984, *Healing as Sacrament: The Sanctification of the World*, London: Darton, Longman and Todd.

Morris Maddocks, 1990, *The Christian Healing Ministry*, London: SPCK.

Ordination

Alan Billings, 2010, *Making God Possible: The Task of Ordained Ministry Present and Future*, London: SPCK.
Christopher Cocksworth and Rosalind Brown, 2002, *Being a Priest Today*, Norwich: Canterbury Press.
Robin Ward, 2011, *On Christian Priesthood*, London: Continuum.

Marriage

Peter Brown, 1989, *The Body and Society: Men, Women and Sexual Renunciation in Early Christianity*, New York: Columbia University Press.
Jack Dominian, 1981, *Marriage, Faith and Love*, London: Darton, Longman and Todd.
Adrian Thatcher, 1999, *Marriage after Modernity: Christian Marriage in Postmodern Times*, New York: University Press.